The

Golden Prayer

Search

The

Golden Prayer

Search

By

Auriel Wyndham Livezey

Mountaintop Publishing

Printed in the United States of America
ISBN 978-1-893930-10-0

Mountaintop Publishing
www.MountaintopPublishing.com

CONTENTS

Introduction 9

About the Journey 19

Part One
Traveling North: the Word............... 27

Part Two
Traveling East: Christ..................... 49

Part Three
Traveling South: Christianity.......... 87

Part Four
Traveling West: Divine Science 151

Golden Glimpses............................ 179

Note

The books of the Bible are not usually abbreviated.
The works of Mary Baker Eddy are abbreviated.
Science and Health with Key to the Scriptures is
often simply S&H followed by the page number.
Miscellaneous Writings is shown as Mis.
First Church of Christ, Scientist and Miscellany
is My.
Retrospection and Introspection is Ret.
Rudimental Divine Science is Rud.
Message to The Mother Church for 1901
becomes Mess. '01.
No and Yes is usually just No.
The Manual of the Mother Church might be Manual
or Man, followed by the page number.
Pulpit and Press is just Pul.
Christian Science versus Pantheism is Pan.

Pilgrim on earth, thy home is heaven; stranger, thou art the guest of God.

Mary Baker Eddy

Introduction

How did we get here?

We arrived at this point by reading about the adventures of Earnest Eager in *The Golden Prayer Puzzle*. Through an unexpected clue, he solved Bible mysteries and found a guided pathway through life. Now, Earnest is about to embark on this new phase of discovery. He, and we too, will follow the clues he finds step by step. There are no shortcuts.

The Golden Prayer Puzzle was actually a process of "follow the clue." Each one was a treasure, especially that one particular construction in language, which is rarely discussed, but is in common usage! Just as a noun, verb, or adjective is neutral until applied, so is the concept of generic and specific. And it solves so many mysteries!

But that was only the beginning. By following the guided pathway, Earnest will make many important discoveries. For instance, there are golden prayer veins sparkling on the north point of his journey. From there on, he finds one nugget after another. Now, you may recall, we last saw Earnest as he was sitting on the deck of the boat, waiting to depart.

* * * * * * * * *

How did I get here?

Earnest Eager pondered that question as he sat on the narrow deck of the boat and watched the river traffic. Suddenly, he saw the same two small speedboats, which had passed by five or six minutes ago. They were still traveling in opposite directions, searching for the gold of prayer. "They must have gone around in a circle," Earnest surmised, as he looked up and down the river for clues. That would mean the land opposite was a small island.

The river was a bit of a mystery to Earnest, but he was patient and would allow for events to take their natural course.

Earnest settled back again to review his day, which had already been so eventful. The early-morning meeting at the skydiving school; the puzzle given them to solve; figuring out the clues; and then his actual journey, seemed to have taken place last week instead of on that very morning. He shook his head in wonder at it all.

On thinking about his fellow skydivers, he was sorry that Selby Selfish had landed in the river and was not continuing on. Then busy Colin Collector was so occupied in gathering ideas from other people that he gave up his own prayer search.

However, Earnest was happy he'd caught a glimpse of Gerald Generic and Spencer Specific in the distance. Evidently they had patched up their differences enough to be on their way together. The argument between them had been of inestimable value to Earnest, and was truly the largest clue of all, helping him solve mysteries in the Guidebook. He had even found a guided pathway through life. Oh, it wasn't that he had spent a great deal of time at the Guidebook kiosk or even at the baseball shop, but the ideas had been so momentous and revelatory, that they filled his thinking and his day. Walking along Life's Highway had provided this sincere seeker with more insights, and time to reflect, until the little chapel on a small hill rose into view. The orientation tour there had been so revealing. "Yes, it's a strange little town," Earnest thought to himself, smiling happily, as he kept pondering.

Suddenly, the noise of other seekers, who were quickly filling up the boat, roused Earnest out of his reverie. Obviously they would all soon depart. A great sense of anticipation almost overwhelmed him. He was about to solve yet another mystery!

* * * * * * * * * *

A momentous event

Along with Earnest, I could well ponder how I got to this point. It had been quite a long trek; one that began in 1980 with a statement my husband Glen made the day after Mt. St. Helens erupted. There was no previous hint of a coming seismic shift in our lives, but it came anyway. This is how it happened.

We'd spent a weekend in Seattle, during which time I'd addressed an all-day meeting of Christian Scientists. Glen was present as a guest, and we thoroughly enjoyed our day with that animated and eager group of students.

We were flying out of Seattle on May 18th and, as our plane was preparing to take off, the large screen in the plane's cabin was showing the latest news—the eruption of the volcano. However, the view on the screen was quickly eclipsed by the real-life scene, as the pilot flew us around the mushroom that was forming in the sky. Everyone in that plane had front-row seats in nature's theater.

In a way, that huge event was a preamble to our own event of some proportion. The very next day, Glen suddenly turned to me and said, "I don't think we've been making a good enough distinction between prayer and treatment." That short sentence started us on a very long journey, one that is still ongoing, even as I write this book thirty-six years later!

Like Earnest's day which was full of amazing lessons, those thirty-six years have been likewise packed full of spiritual adventures. Opportunities to share what Glen and I discovered, or rather uncovered, were plentiful. We gave day-long addresses each year and church talks, not to mention the individual sharing that took place in our practice of Christian Science. Over the years, since Glen's passing in 1993, I continued this sharing.

In 2008, I gave a talk to a group of Christian Science nurses on the subject of prayer. The talk had fallen automatically into four parts. That was how it later went out as a four-part newsletter to churches and dedicated workers in the field of Christian Science. The last issue promised a book to come in 2009, but that did not occur. However, with more questions arising on the subject, everything points to this now being the right time for a book.

So, let's return to Glen's statement about prayer and treatment. I don't know what triggered this recognition. Perhaps it came from Glen's early years as a Quaker, or even the next few years as a Methodist. That period was followed by a religious vacuum in his adult life, until an overnight healing of a severe back problem catapulted him into the study of Christian Science.

The treatment, to which Glen referred, was Christian Science treatment. We had both been employed as practitioners in this healing ministry since the 1960s, so we were not without experience in that field. Many wonderful results had come about during those years, so you may wonder why we hadn't known, or why it seemed so important now, to understand the difference between prayer and treatment. Actually, we weren't sure ourselves what it would mean, but we soon found out.

To begin with, it was common practice for us, and many other students of Christian Science, to make the quick explanation to an inquirer that a Christian

Science practitioner healed through prayer. After Glen's statement, and our consequent prayer journey, we came to realize just how necessary it was for us, and for those seeking an explanation, to be more accurate, much more specific.

With patience, we pondered this subject deeply. Were we using the term *prayer* as a type of generic or fit-all statement to refer to turning to God? And did this usage muddy the understanding of both prayer and treatment? We quickly discovered the answer was "yes." Like detectives on the trail to solve a case, we followed a number of clues. The next clue was another question.

If it was actually true that prayer and Christian Science treatment were two different spiritual concepts or activities, why had we not seen this sooner? In the process of unraveling the intertwined verbiage and coming to grips with the terms, we quickly found out why.

Again, it was Glen who made the telling comment, "We would know more about *Science and Health* if we'd taken it for one semester in college, than we do now after studying it for decades." It seemed we had not been well enough prepared, or perhaps not thorough enough in our studies.

Added to the irony of our situation was the fact that we had, years before we even knew each other, written articles on those very subjects. Glen's article, "Preparation" was published in the *Christian Science Sentinel* in 1969, and one of mine titled, "Are

We Thorough Enough?" appeared in *The Christian Science Journal* in 1973.

With the recognition that we were always learning in this earthly school, we could easily see that third-grade thoroughness and preparation differ greatly from the eleventh or twelfth grade. So, we set about to grow in our understanding. After all, *Science and Health* page 10 contained this statement: "The world must grow to the spiritual understanding of prayer."

The next logical question emerged. How had we been studying this precious Science of the Christ? Well, for years we had relied heavily on daily study of the weekly Bible Lesson-Sermon, which was also read in Christian Science churches around the world on Sunday. Twenty-six topics cover so many subjects, reaching far beyond religious questions such as, "Christ Jesus," or "Doctrine of Atonement" to ones that could be in a medical or scientific classification. In other words, they would be of interest to those in the fields of science, theology, or medicine.

Indeed, the Bible has broad application. There is a Bible Lesson denouncing hypnotism, for instance, and others are titled, "God the Preserver of Man," and "Are Sin, Disease, and Death Real?" Also included is the thought-provoking scientific query, "Is the Universe, Including Man, Evolved by Atomic Force?" The seeker of Truth will find the presentation geared to their particular need or interest.

A specific example of this might be helpful. A friend told me that when a woman wanted to visit her

Christian Science church one Sunday, the Lesson for that week was "Everlasting Punishment." My friend said she shuddered at the thought that this woman's first introduction to Christian Science would be that particular subject, for it could sound unkind at first glance. The woman had recently lost her husband, so the Lesson "Love" might be more comforting.

In addition, the woman's husband had been criticized as not having been saved according to the religion of his family. As it turned out, "Everlasting Punishment" was the one the visitor needed. It showed, through the Bible and *Science and Health*, that God's love is everlasting and freely given to all, and contains no membership requirement in a certain brand of Christianity.

Furthermore, if we need to reform our ways, there is still no such thing as punishment that lasts forever, for we all have the right, here and hereafter, to make corrections or U-turns in our lives. Any particular punishment we bring on ourselves would last only as long as the wrongdoing. That particular Lesson-Sermon was indeed the perfect one for the newcomer to hear. It answered a perplexing, theological question for her.

These Lesson-Sermons are carefully prepared. An expert and dedicated Bible Lesson Committee compile citations from the Bible and *Science and Health* for subjects chosen by Mary Baker Eddy.

However, something became very clear, as Glen and I further pursued the idea of study. Though the content of these Lessons is *in context* with the subject for that week, it is actually *out of context* with the books themselves.

Here was the crux of our problem. Each chapter of *Science and Health* has its own subject, and if we were diligent college students, with that book as a textbook, we would surely thoroughly explore its contents chapter by chapter. Glen and I saw that we didn't really have a good grasp on most of the chapters in *Science and Health*, only the excerpts from them. We needed to thoroughly study each chapter by finding its thesis or main statement, and by exploring the explanations that followed.

Next was the need to unravel any confusion between prayer and treatment. Therefore, the work of the moment was to delve specifically into the chapter titled, "Prayer" in which that subject was dealt with, and the one on "Christian Science Practice," in which treatment was discussed and illustrated. The books started to open up for us!

Our increased appreciation for the wholeness of the books removed any ritualized sense of the Lesson we had entertained. That false sense had confined us and even the books themselves. The Bible and *Science and Health* had been ordained by Mrs. Eddy as Pastor for the Christian Science churches. Obviously, any pastor has a lot more to say to his flock than the Sunday Sermon, and we needed to allow that ministering to take place in our lives.

One may wonder, at this point, if the Bible Lessons took a back seat. In fact, the opposite occurred. They actually took on new meaning. It was a few years later that we put our thoughts down in a short piece titled, "One week's good news." This writing explored how applicable the Lesson of the week was to the news of that week. Far more than an individual study and application, we saw how the Lesson could also tackle local and world issues.

Yes, the Lesson broadened its appeal, became more general, as our own study of the Bible and *Science and Health* became more focused and specific. Up to that point, we had simply possessed a Gerald Generic perspective of those books, and we really needed to add the Spencer Specific touch.

We didn't know then, but the search for the gold of prayer had begun! I'll be drawing on the results of our search for this book and will explain along the way just how our lives and others were impacted by that one simple observation—"I don't think we've been making a good enough distinction between prayer and treatment."

We're ready to travel now, but before we board our own boat of discovery, let's take just a moment to talk about the overall concept and purpose of life's journey.

About the Journey

Where does the guided pathway, which Earnest Eager found at the baseball shop, lead us? As we traverse it many times, increasingly rising higher, we'll finally arrive at the amazing scene that St. John saw through spiritual sense alone. He "became conscious of the spiritual facts of being." (S&H 574) The Book of Revelation records John's view of an entirely spiritual creation—the reality, which had been prophesied by Isaiah, and termed the new heaven and new earth.

Mary Baker Eddy asked if we could imagine such a sublime scene: "Have you ever pictured this heaven and earth, inhabited by beings under the control of supreme wisdom?" (S&H 90)

In the new world, there would be no more pain, sorrow, or partings. You'd think there would be a rush to arrive there, but let's look in on a group of dedicated, spiritual thinkers.

When the speaker at a church inspirational meeting asked the lively and interested audience a certain question, there was total silence. One woman tentatively raised her hand, and another one slowly followed. A moment later, both retracted their agreement. The first gave no explanation, but the second woman mumbled something about having grandchildren. Nervous laughter rippled throughout the audience and then, once again, silence prevailed. What was the question? It was a very simple one and a supposed expectation or hope of sincere Christians. The speaker asked: "Who would be willing to ascend today, if that were possible?" Obviously, the idea was not very appealing.

Lest we feel somewhat guilty for not desiring to ascend right now, we may recall the period between Jesus' resurrection and his ascension. He had to give up the sense of matter as substance and wait until "spiritual sense had quenched all earthly yearnings." (S&H 313)

The relinquishment of all earthly ties was a necessary step before he could leave the material, human, mortal scene for the spiritual, divine, immortal reality. And yet he was well acquainted with that new heaven and earth. It's understandable that the rest of us, being rather unacquainted, might be a trifle hesitant.

Of course, we probably don't need to worry about choosing to ascend or not at this point of our spiritual development, though a humorous piece was published (as I recall, in the Readers' Digest) after the large annual meeting of a church. A pair of shoes stood all by themselves in one aisle, which prompted the remark, "Well, somebody made it!"

No, our actual ascension is not the question of the moment though, in a way of course, we are all truly ascending daily, if we follow the path of the Christ, Truth. It happens rather automatically.

John saw the New Jerusalem. That city foursquare was pure gold "and the street of the city was pure gold, as it were transparent glass." (Rev. 22:18,21) What beautiful symbolism and imagery to describe how precious spiritual understanding is!

As we explore the way to that city foursquare, we'll find many instances of heaven on earth. This is not too ethereal to imagine. No huge leap is necessary and no hard-to-make decision. We can stay with and enjoy the grandchildren for awhile yet.

It isn't wrong, or selfish, for us to want to experience harmony, health and joy in abundance, as long as we desire it for everyone else too. Actually, Christ Jesus gave us that petition as part of his prayer. *Science and Health* on page 17, provides the spiritual sense and specifics of the request.

Thy will be done in earth, as it is in heaven.
Enable us to know, — as in heaven, so on earth,
— God is omnipotent, supreme.

Jesus had us pray for heaven on earth, which is on the way to the new heaven and earth and New Jerusalem. As we compared the sides and the points of the city in *The Golden Prayer Puzzle*, we found they were almost identical, except the points enlarged upon the sides. That's why it seemed logical to conclude that the sides were generic descriptions and the points were specific ones, filling in the details. Let's look at them again together.

"The four sides of our city are: the Word, Christ, Christianity, and divine Science." (S&H 575)

The "four cardinal points are: first, the Word of Life, Truth and Love; second, the Christ, the spiritual idea of God; third, Christianity, which is the outcome of the divine Principle of the Christ-idea in Christian history; fourth, Christian Science, which to-day and forever interprets this great example and the great Exemplar." (S&H 577)

As mentioned in the previous book, there will be no attempt to entertain other interpretations of the city foursquare than those given in *Science and Health*. It would be obviously wise, however, to observe and apply all that is said, but without abstract or involved reasoning. Let's keep it simple and according to our textbooks!

We'll travel the sides of the city, and touch each point. Stars, described on page 575, provide us with the directions of a spiritually-symbolic compass, and also shed light on the human pathway. They are the North Star; the Bethlehem star of the East; the Southern Cross to the south; and lastly, in the daylight, we reach the western Golden Shore of Love with the Peaceful Sea of Harmony. We have sides, points and stars for our journey. That is our itinerary, and that is sufficient!

With such a clearly defined itinerary, we're not left wandering around in a strange land, but are pilgrims on a guided expedition to the holiest of all lands—our own true state of being and the understanding of the spiritual universe, which God has created. That's our heaven and our true home. Mary Baker Eddy told us a secret about herself when she admitted, "I am constantly homesick for heaven." (Mis. 177)

If you have ever felt a strong longing for somewhere, but don't know where, you may be heavenly homesick. In that case, the journey around the city foursquare should speak to you.

One of Mrs. Eddy's favorite hymns was written by her contemporary, Mary S. B. Dana Shindler. How poignantly the lyrics show the yearning and expectation of that religious era. Here is the first verse of hymn 415 in the *Christian Science Hymnal:*

> I'm a pilgrim, and I'm a stranger;
> I can tarry, I can tarry but a night.
> Do not detain me, for I am going
> To where the fountains are ever flowing:
> Refrain
> I'm a pilgrim, and I'm a stranger;
> I can tarry, I can tarry but a night.

Regarding our journey, Mrs. Eddy reassured us: "Pilgrim on earth, thy home is heaven; stranger, thou are the guest of God." (S&H 254)

The prophets and great Bible characters were certainly pilgrims, and they knew it. They truly recognized, along with Paul, that they had a spiritual race to run and a goal to reach.

However, it seems that it was not only the men who were traveling. An amazing thought suddenly appeared when I was reading about Mary, the mother of Jesus, in a Bible reference book. It stated that she appeared only four times after Jesus began his ministry. Could Mary have gone around the city foursquare? That was my question and, after a little research, this is what I found. Yes, she had!

Mary was present, and even prepared the way for him, when Jesus turned the water into wine (the **Word** he spoke was with power). Her next appearance was in the company of other family members, wanting to speak with Jesus as he was preaching. On hearing that, Jesus referred to those who desired to hear and do the will of God as his family. He was reminding them of the **Christ**, the spiritual idea of sonship. Mary's presence at the cross must have been extremely difficult, but she was there at that ultimate sacrifice, the emblem of **Christianity**. Finally, we find Mary waiting with the disciples and others for the appearance of the Holy Ghost, **divine Science,** on the day of Pentecost.

Those are the four parts. When viewed as a whole, the city foursquare, New Jerusalem, is: "Divine Science; the understanding of the spiritual facts and harmony of the universe." (S&H 592)

Here again is an example of the generic and the specific. Divine Science is the name for New Jerusalem and it is also a specific part of that city.

In the same way, that city is our destination and the way there. Physically speaking, that would make no sense. The city is the way to the city? But, it's a spiritually mental state we are aiming for, and obviously we gain understanding step by step. "Perfection is gained only by perfection." (S&H 290)

Thinking of the whole or the big picture, let's look again at our spiritual destination and pathway.

The new heaven and earth is a divine, not human, state of being. "The divine understanding reigns, is all, and there is no other consciousness." (S&H 536)

Heaven on earth is a transitional stage, where the divine truths of heaven appear on earth bringing harmony with them. Human consciousness is still in evidence, but is becoming enlightened by Truth. This progressive stage of spiritual development is attained by means of prayer understood and practiced, as we travel around the city foursquare. With that in mind, let's turn our attention to the journey itself and questions travelers might have.

Over the years I've found, and much to my dismay, that one cannot answer a question that someone doesn't have. But, students of Christian Science are asking: How do we accomplish better healing? What is happening to the churches today? *The Golden Prayer Puzzle* touched on the first question, and this volume will include both subjects.

Of course, that's rather like dessert, which many would prefer as their main or starting course. It is humbly recommended that in this restaurant of ideas, with a menu that has been prepared for you after years of studying the recipe books, that you not hurry your meal to reach dessert. There are many courses that need careful digestion, and which will make dessert much more meaningful and fulfilling. Yes, this journey is multi-faceted!

As in Volume 1 of these golden prayer books, the Bible, containing the "recipe for all healing" (S&H 406) is our Guidebook and *Science and Health* is the book with the key to those sacred Scriptures.

Prior to boarding, you may like to review the travel plans that Earnest found at the baseball shop in *The Golden Prayer Puzzle*.

You will also find it helpful to open to those explanatory passages, on pages 575 and 577 of *Science and Health with Key to the Scriptures* by Mary Baker Eddy.

Now, with our itinerary clearly in mind, let's join our intrepid traveler. He is so earnest and eager in his desire to find the gold of prayer, and hopes to be in the company of others who are like minded. Perhaps, someone like you!

PART ONE

Traveling North: the Word

Finding prayer through the Word

Earnest Eager heard some surprising news. The public address system on the boat was announcing that the expedition would begin by slowly circling around the small island to the north of them. During that time, the group would listen to lessons regarding prayer as found specifically in the Word of the Guidebook with help from the Key book. They would hold their course for awhile, following their North Star of inquiry, and then they would travel the eastern river.

It was further explained that the orientation tour had actually served as the first leg of the journey, with the more general approach to prayer.

Earnest knew that the Word as found in the Guidebook was invaluable, no matter what the subject at hand was to be studied. He even surmised correctly that different aspects of prayer would be examined on this trip, so he made a note of the fact that his first gold nugget was the idea of praying to, or asking, the Supreme Being. And he was keenly aware that he must watch for the general idea, and the specifics of that idea, on each leg of his journey. As for the rest, well, the stars and the baseball diamond would make his path clear. Earnest even quietly verbalized that to himself, as he watched the boat crew cast off the moorings. With a blast of its horn, the boat slowly set off to sail around the island.

Anticipation and inquiring expressions were on all faces, so questions and answers immediately began to take shape.

* * * * * * * * * *

Since 1980, there have been numerous opportunities to take others on the prayer route that Glen and I traveled, and which I continued to travel after his passing. The reactions of travelers were quite varied, and questions or challenges inevitably arose. It is hoped this trip will incorporate enough of those queries to satisfy this present group of prayer seekers. Each time I sail this stream of thought, there is always something new to be seen and more spiritual ground to be gained.

The journey took on an increasingly defined pathway, over the years, through the understanding of the city foursquare in the book of Revelation. That book was termed "The Apocalypse" around the year 1150 A.D. and the meaning of it is an "uncovering," or "disclosing." How appropriate that is for our prayer search! Beautiful concepts, shining like jewels through the pages of the Bible or *Science and Health*, could be covered up over time due to misunderstanding, misuse or simply the changing of eras. Those jewels would then become buried treasure, which needs to be found and uncovered. That was how Glen and I approached our search for the gold of prayer.

As previously mentioned in *The Golden Prayer Puzzle*, the city foursquare begins to structure our own individual search for truth, even when we are not totally aware this is happening. This was the case with the *Bird* book, and with the four-part newsletters on prayer. When we do become conscious of that fact, we look for that pattern in our everyday lives. That's the reason this book and journey will be structured that way.

Feel free on this trip to pause as many times as necessary to consult the resource materials. Nothing voiced on our journey, or in this book, should be taken as truth unless backed up thoroughly and consistently in the Guidebook, and our Key book, *Science and Health with Key to the Scriptures*, including the *Prose Works* of Mary Baker Eddy.

A word of caution: Glen and I found that it's not sufficient to take one quotation as agreement for our own hypotheses. In fact, a whole new teaching has sometimes arisen in exactly that fashion. There will always be 95% of the references to any subject in those books that point in a certain direction. The other few percent, that appear to travel in a different direction, can be left safely on the back burner of thought, until they bubble to the surface and become plain to us. Let's look at an example.

Mrs. Eddy's statement, "Petitions bring to mortals only the results of mortals' own faith," (S&H 11) has sometimes been used to devalue petition, even to discredit petitioning God altogether. On careful examination, we find it is not the petition that is in doubt or in question, but rather our own faith. If we read all the citations in these works (and Glen and I did) we'll find that petition is not only in vogue or acceptable but absolutely necessary to our spiritual progress and to experiencing a closeness with God.

So again, please don't take this book's word on prayer, but let's consult thoroughly with the Word of God. No earthly degree, or human rank, is high enough to take the place of the heavenly-revealed truth. This kind of research will take some effort and concentration. It's far easier to ask someone else's opinion as did Colin Collector, but our own research is so rewarding and, when totally honest, it will keep us on track.

Finding prayer

The orientation tour prior to boarding provided us with a general idea of prayer. We'll now circle around the north point of the city by considering what prayer specifically is as revealed through the Word of Life, Truth and Love. The North Star, also called Polaris, had long been the sailors' lifeline, as they aligned with this celestial light. It was their point of reference keeping them on course. The North Star in modern times is often used to refer symbolically to an alignment, often a moral one. The Word of God is our North Star.

Now, it is usual to take the meaning of prayer more or less for granted, so it might be worth thinking over how one would describe prayer to someone else and comparing our concept with the Bible. If we are sincerely unprejudiced and willing to retrace our steps when necessary, we'll find pure gold. It is with this agreement that we board our boat. As the moorings are cast off, our deliberations immediately begin.

We first discover that the Bible contains 513 references to forms of the word *pray*, and it appears that approximately two-thirds of these are in the Old Testament. Now, here's the interesting thing: So many of them refer to asking someone for pardon or a favor, "Give me, I pray thee, a little water to drink..." (Judges 4:19). The rest refer to asking God, "So Abraham prayed unto God: and God healed Abimelech..." (Genesis 20:17). The Old English polite form of asking was the word *pray*. This is no longer commonly or even casually used in conversation unless we humorously exclaim to a friend, "Oh, you have a secret? Pray, do tell!" However, the usage still lingers in the legal profession, where this formal request is commonplace: "Plaintiff prays for judgment against the Defendants." Obviously the word *pray* carries more gravitas than *ask*. Then a shift occurs. In the New Testament, the proportion changes from mainly asking individuals to asking God. Yes, the majority of the references to prayer pertain to turning to God and petitioning Him: "O my Father, if it be possible, let this cup pass from me. . ." (Matthew 26:39). Nowhere does it appear that the asking, the desiring or requesting, is taken out of prayer. That's the basic meaning of the word,—"to ask." The definition has not changed since the time of Mary Baker Eddy and in so many languages it denotes an earnest petition or supplication to God. That is how the Bible treats the subject. Mary Baker Eddy prayed the same way.

> Each day I pray: "God bless my enemies; make them Thy friends; give them to know the joy and the peace of love." (*First Church of Christ, Scientist and Miscellany*, 220)

Humanity had prayed all throughout the centuries, so obviously Mary Baker Eddy did not discover prayer. But her discovery of a Biblically-based "metaphysical system of treating disease" gave prayer a whole new standing and impetus.

At this point we are all still together, and our boat is on an even keel. Let's try out just one sentence from *Science and Health,* and see what happens. In the chapter, "Christian Science Practice," is a paragraph heading "Aids in Sickness" beside three sentences, which discuss how a nurse should aid a patient. Here's one sentence on page 395.

"Prayers, in which God is not asked to heal but is besought to take the patient to Himself, do not benefit the sick." Does that rock our boat a bit? Of course, it's well to remember Mrs. Eddy's times, and that it was common for people (perhaps it still is for some) to ask God to take the sufferer to Himself. That sounds more like an exit line than a healing one and was obviously not helpful in Mrs. Eddy's eyes. She basically warns us of it and shows the more beneficial way, which is to ask God to heal the sick. Here's one pause point on our journey, as we ponder this question: How comfortable are we with asking God to heal the sick? But, it's an aid in sickness. Are we willing to give this aid? That might be a logical question. And, if not, why not?

The first statement in the chapter "Prayer" in *Science and Health*, explains the prayer that heals. It's as though someone had asked the silent question (in a way Christians had long been doing that very thing): "What is the kind of prayer that is effective and that reforms and heals?" The discoverer of Christian Science had already proved her answer so could confidently state the following.

> The prayer that reforms the sinner
> and heals the sick is an absolute faith
> that all things are possible to God,—a
> spiritual understanding of Him, an
> unselfed love. (S&H 1)

Let's note that Mrs. Eddy is not redefining the word *prayer*, but is pointing to the prayer that really works—the one that is effective—"the prayer that reforms the sinner and heals the sick." The elements of this prayer, this asking, require no deep understanding of Mrs. Eddy's metaphysical system of treating disease. The closest it may come is the mention of a "spiritual understanding of Him."

But many have approximated that spiritual understanding, if we read the literature of our day, and their prayers do heal. Perhaps we could even say they have gained the generic sense of prayer through the Word, and some of the specifics found in Christian Science. They have approximated "the understanding of Christian Science sufficiently to heal the sick in his name." (Pul. 22)

The leaven of Christian Science has been at work for a century and a half, and references to God as Spirit, as divine Mind, or divine Love are quite frequent, as are statements that God does not send ill-health. We hear accounts of Christian churches and groups praying for others most unselfishly and having good success.

A Christian search

A meeting at a Lutheran Church, in the 1980s, stands out vividly in my memory. Glen and I had attended a special, open meeting to hear the pastor, a man with an incredible sense of humor, describe how he and his church members had searched for the prayer that heals. They were so dedicated and sincere. He said they had tried everything, even standing in the different corners of the church while praying.

Well, one day their consecrated prayers and deep faith were rewarded, for they were able to heal someone with a gangrenous leg. What joy they felt! And what great, unselfed love they had exhibited in their perseverance to find the prayer that heals.

In her *Message to The Mother Church* in 1901, Mary Baker Eddy speaks of the Christians and clergymen of her day, and not only approves of but loves their doctrine of prayer:

> Christians and clergymen pray for sinners; they believe that God answers their prayers, and that prayer is a divinely appointed means of grace and salvation. They believe that divine power, besought, is given to them in times of trouble, and that He worketh with them to save sinners. I love this doctrine, for I know that prayer brings the seeker into closer proximity with

divine Love, and thus he finds what he seeks, the power of God to heal and to save. Jesus said, "Ask, and ye shall receive;" and if not immediately, continue to ask, and because of your often coming it shall be given unto you; and he illustrated his saying by a parable. (p. 18)

Here is the crux of the matter, the point of the gold. Mary Baker Eddy never removed the asking, requests, or petition from prayer. That would be like taking the ice out of the ice-cream! She did show there was more to this prayer than simply asking God and hoping for His favor. We'll delve into that a little later on during our expedition, but for now let's consider the asking aspect.

Resistance to asking

The human mind appears to possess an unreasonable reluctance to asking, which was humorously illustrated in a *Christian Science Sentinel* cartoon of Moses' Moving Co. It depicted a caravan of moving vans and a bejeweled woman saying to the driver, the bearded man beside her, "It's been 40 YEARS! Maybe we should stop and ask for directions." Right there is the catch! Asking takes humility.

No, ladies, it's not always the gentlemen who don't like to ask for directions. How well I remember buying a new vacuum cleaner that boasted it would adjust to the height of the carpet by a simple turn of a knob. Mine wouldn't turn, no matter how much pressure I exerted on it. Finally, I obeyed the old adage, "When all else fails, read the directions." The answer was quick and simple. The vacuum needed to be tilted slightly and then the little knob moved like butter melting on a hot skillet. The tilt, the attitude, of the vacuum had to be right, and evidently so does ours. Humility is the attitude that invites and accepts the answer we need. Asking our divine Principle, Love, indicates not only humility but also that we trust God. We don't doubt that He knows. Rather, it implies that *we* don't know. In other words: He knows. We don't. We ask!

It should be as simple as that, but it isn't. Human thought has ingeniously come up with all the reasons we shouldn't ask from "It's not metaphysical, so simply declare what you know" to "If God knows all then I shouldn't need to ask, because He is already supplying my need." Yes, God is supplying our need, but the problem is we don't always see it. That's why we ask, even as Elisha prayed for his servant's eyes to be opened to the truth, so he could recognize the protection around them. The need was already met, but he hadn't seen it.

If loving parents had prepared a sumptuous graduation party for their children, and all that could possibly be needed was provided on that table, there still might be questions regarding the specifics. Someone might say, "Well, I know the salt is on the table somewhere, but I just can't find it. Would you point it out to me, please?" Even before the question, the provision was there.

Jesus knew that all good is as ever present as God is. "Your Father knoweth what things ye have need of, before ye ask Him." (Matthew 6:8) So, why did Jesus tell us to ask? "Ask and it shall be given you, seek and ye shall find, knock and it shall be opened." Ask, seek, and knock. A-S-K. It wasn't for God's sake or to test Him, but for *our* sake. Prayer brings us closer to God, ("into closer proximity with divine Love") so we may hear the answers we need. Moving closer to hear a communication makes good sense on both a human and a divine level.

Turning to God, the divine Mind, for answers is a basic acknowledgment that there is a higher power, a supreme intelligence, to which we may resort. (This was dealt with during the Orientation Tour.) Making statements of truth does not necessarily admit that fact. There is a subtle resistance to talking with God, as it requires that admission of a power we cannot see. Can we communicate with that which is invisible to human eyes? That's the question and that is the challenge.

This subject will come up again on the next leg of our journey. For now, let's keep exploring the asking territory.

Mental territory

Through prayer we see more of heaven on earth. Why is that? It's because asking God to heal the sick is basically asking for the heaven of health and harmony to be made evident on the human scene. "Enable us to know, – as in heaven, so on earth."

Because prayer is addressed to God and not aimed at anyone, not trying to correct certain errors in a person's thinking or even calm their fears, it needs no permission.

Arguments regarding another's well being tend to put one in the lawyer's shoes, and this does need permission, even as a lawyer doesn't argue a case without being hired to do so. Prayer, asking God, is the safest way to make sure one is not invading another's mental territory.

The solution of clearing one's own thought will often come up as the best way of helping others. People often call this prayer. Strictly speaking, it does not fall into that category.

Oh, there's no doubt that consciousness, filled with the divine facts of being, such as perfect God and perfect man, will benefit others. But those facts must be kept general. If one becomes specific in this knowing, it borders on treating a case. This is where prayer comes to the rescue and allows us to aid anyone, anytime. We may pray for a loved one, for their health, their well-being, their joy and success. A nurse may pray for a patient, while the practitioner gives Christian Science treament. And of course, we should pray for the government and for our enemies too.

Right at this point there are usually murmurs of concern about the direction our journey is taking. Let's pause for a few moments to ponder the subject further by an examination of the two chapters that Glen and I studied in order to solve the mystery of prayer and treatment.

Two distinct chapters

Our first foray into the land of prayer and treatment will surely bear immediate fruit with this group, as it did with Glen and me. We quickly find there are so many terms, such as: desire, longing, yearning, aspirations, requests, asking, petition, plus over seventy references to various forms of the word *pray* in the seventeen pages of the chapter, 'Prayer." However, there is absolutely no mention of treatment, patients, practitioners, or arguing a case.

On the other hand, the chapter, "Christian Science Practice" contains no discussion of prayer. The term is used only three times, and that chapter is one of the longest in the book. A section titled "Mental treatment illustrated," however, is a prominent part of the chapter on practice.

Though there are over seventy references to prayer in that first short chapter, Mrs. Eddy uses forms of the word *pray* only thirty-two more times over the remainder of the whole book. The proportion tells its own tale. The largest clue to prayer is in the chapter named for it. After this kind of research, there is usually not one objection to stating the obvious fact, that "Prayer" and "Christian Science Practice" are two different chapters and subjects. To reinforce the concept of such distinctions on our spiritual landscape, we turn to the group.

Our passengers are asked about their favorite activities—the physical activities that require some exertion. Many answers come back immediately. Some like dancing, jogging, walking, hiking, tennis, skating, horseback riding, swimming, soccer and surfing.

The list promises to go indefinitely, and it's best to call a halt with another question. What spiritual activities do you enjoy? A few people will usually answer that they enjoy pondering spiritual truths, understanding, knowing, declaring, keeping the truth in mind, arguing the facts, and going to God in prayer.

We can readily see that there are many specifics under the general heading of spiritual activities, just as there are under the heading of physical activities. The details do make a difference in both cases.

With the agreement that prayer is not only communicating with but freely asking God, we have arrived at an important point. It's our first excursion into the outer rim of the gold mine and actual prayer. Let's test it for its gold content.

Testing our prayer. Is it real? Or, is it "Fool's Gold" we have found?

How do we know if our prayer, our asking, is correct? Is there a litmus test for prayer? Yes, there is and I faced that test in a Laundromat of all places. What's more, I was flunking! Here is what happened.

It promised to be a peaceful time as I tackled my laundry. No one else was there, so I could think and pray. Then, a young mother with two little ones came in. The baby in the stroller seemed very uncomfortable and was crying pitifully, while the toddler yanked on the stroller now and then, which didn't help matters at all.

Grumbling a little over the disruption, I came to the conclusion that I should at least pray for the baby's peace. I began to pray but in a rather half-hearted way: "Dear Father, may this child feel Your peace. . ." or words to that effect.

Suddenly, in the middle of my request, I stopped and realized that I wasn't praying for the child's peace at all. I was the one who wanted the peace and quiet. That's when I knew my prayer was failing the test. It was actually "fool's gold"– prayer that seemed genuine but wasn't. I was simply fooling myself.

How did I know that? It was because of what page 9 in *Science and Health* states.

The test of all prayer lies in the answer to these questions: Do we love our neighbor better because of this asking? Do we pursue the old selfishness, satisfied with having prayed for something better, though we give no evidence of the sincerity of our requests by living consistently with our prayer?

(Notice how Mrs. Eddy classes not just some but *all* prayer as asking or requesting.)

What a sobering thing to find that my so-called prayer would only have me loving myself better but not my neighbor. So more humbly I prayed again, "Dear Father, may this child feel the peace and health that are present right here and now. May no material circumstance rob it of any of the good You have provided. . . ." Suddenly all was quiet, for the baby was peacefully asleep and remained that way for the rest of the time there. However, it wasn't the child's reaction that tested my prayer but the love for my neighbor.

The general consciousness of God's goodness would undoubtedly have blessed that situation, but I could do something specific. I could do something very active for the child. I could pray! This prayer was the desire to see "as in heaven, so on earth" for that sweet child. And it was so!

What about all the knowing we do, the declaring of truths and the arguments we make, which we have learned in Christian Science? Well, they too are facets of spiritual thinking that is turned Godward. Whether silent or audible, each one varies to some degree from the other. They are all different types of spiritual gems, and all are precious. So how does prayer fit in here?

Other gems

Let's take a peek at the discovery room on Earnest's boat and look at a showcase of rings that are on display. Each ring has a gold setting.

There is a topaz ring, a ruby ring, and a diamond ring. Finally there is a solid gold ring. The placard indicates these rings are types of spiritual thinking and activity, and all are set in the gold of true desire. We might call the topaz ring the declaring-the-truth ring. For example, when an accident happens, *Science and Health* counsels us: "Declare you are not hurt and understand the reason why..." (397).

The ruby ring might be the arguments-of-truth ring, as when giving Christian Science treatment. "Argue at first mentally, not audibly, that the patient has no disease, and conform the argument so as to destroy the evidence of disease." (S&H 412)

Knowing what is true might be seen as a diamond ring. "Know, then, that you possess sovereign power to think and act rightly, and that nothing can dispossess you of this heritage and trespass on Love." (Pul.3)

However, we would call these rings by the name of the stone, not by their setting.

Only the purely gold ring is specifically referred to as prayer. "Then, in speechless prayer, ask God to enable you to reflect God..." (My. 150)

There are also a few rings without a gold setting. Those are labeled, "vain repetitions." There is no true desire with the gems in these rings, no matter how holy the words may sound. And because they are vain repetitions, they will not transfer over into deeds. We don't put into action that which we don't truly desire. That's a given!

Just asking God isn't enough as this statement shows. "Simply asking that we may love God will never make us love Him; but the longing to be better and holier, expressed in daily watchfulnesss and in striving to assimilate more of the divine character, will mould and fashion us anew, until we awake in His likeness." (S&H 4) That likeness is what Jesus proved and showed to us, and he paid dearly to do it. We follow him by having the right desire, "the longing to be better and holier," and by "striving to assimilate more of the divine character." That's prayer put into action. Desire it; ask for it; do it!

As Glen and I explored the prayer territory, it became obvious that the term *treatment* had been placed as a sub-category of *prayer*, not given its true place as a specific subject on its own. Thus, treatment became a shadow of prayer. This muddied both. Prayer lost its basic ingredient of desire to commune with God and increasingly took on the form of statements and declarations, or even arguments of truth. But those arguments belonged to Christian Science treatment, which in turn was now named prayer. Using the two subjects interchangeably only served to confuse them.

We've heard how precise Mrs. Eddy was with her discovery, and even the details of her home right down to her pincushion. Let's think of *Science and Health* as a metaphysical pincushion with 18 pins in it (18 chapters). If two pins were removed and replaced with only one pin, that would be a loss. By combining the concepts of prayer and treatment, this is essentially what happened.

How did this come about? That's the question that will often arise on any prayer expedition, when the specifics are revealed. A few people will call out that they weren't taught like that. Others want to be sure they are not being misled, and amidst this confusion the boat is rocking a little.

Yes, Glen and I experienced some "rocky" times while sharing these distinctions. But, it's never a question of "who is right," but rather, "what is right."

We are almost at the end of the first stage of circling the north. Let's consider the main point we've learned thus far. Researching the Word found in the Bible and *Science and Health*, reveals that prayer is a direct communication with God.

In this scientific era, awash in information and mass communication, we find that human, mortal reasoning would persuade us by pseudo metaphysics not to ask God, or even to talk with God. "Just affirm what you want and you'll get it" is what the public is being told. But prayer is our vital link to our Maker. Let's continue to pray for ourselves and others and check the result by making sure we pass the test and have more love for our neighbor than ever before.

Now, the full impact of this may not hit all at once. In fact, you may even wonder why so much is being made of asking God. It sounds so simple doesn't it! But it takes work to draw our concept of prayer into line with the Bible and the teachings of *Science and Health*. And the North Star is all about aligning with the Word of God. Without alignment, we'd be traveling in the darkness of a starless night!

Glen and I knew that following the light of Truth and finding this treasure would somehow change everything. And it did! And you will also be amazed at what takes place in your life.

To really appreciate these concepts, it would be helpful to dig further into prayer in the Bible and all that Mary Baker Eddy has to say on petition and asking. Perhaps list each *do* and each *don't* in the chapter "Prayer," and ponder the Daily Prayer and the five petitions that are in it. *Miscellaneous Writings*, page 127, which speaks of asking importunately, provides a large clue for our treasure hunt.

We'll see why asking importunately as Christ Jesus told us to do, and which Mrs. Eddy reiterated, is quite different from pleading with God to do something for us. We'll view how and why petition works, as we enter the second phase of our journey titled, "Our connection to God through prayer." Part three explores, "Prayer for others and sacrifice too!" Lastly, part four rounds out our trip with "Understanding life lessons through prayer."

It's true we don't ask a corporeal God; we don't try to change the Mind of God; we don't ask for frivolous things or to be forgiven while we continue doing wrong, but let's be sure of one great fact. . . we do ask! We're not timid explorers mooring our boat to the dock, reluctant to travel the stream of petition, for there's a great and beautiful journey ahead. We'll have many experiences of heaven on earth on the way to the new heaven and new earth.

As we take the turn in the river, we humbly make four requests, "Thou, Soul, inspiring — Give us vision clear, Break earth-bound fetters, sweep away the veil, Show the new heaven and earth that shall prevail. Alleluia! Alleluia! (Christian Science Hymnal, 66).

PART TWO

Traveling East: the Christ

Our Connection to God through prayer

Earnest Eager was totally delighted by the first stage of the cruise on the river of prayer. He had already made careful note of the fact that he should pray to the Supreme Being. Now he could add the prayer test—finding out if his petitions were genuine prayer—to his list of gold nuggets.

He had looked the showcase of rings over carefully, figuring out the difference. They were all distinct, which helped him to recognize that prayer was also distinct from other kinds of holy thinking. Earnest added this as a gold nugget to his list.

Others around him were on a different track. "You've got to be well connected to find precious gems like these," was a comment that resonated with some. One passenger even wanted to try on the rings and seemed immersed in her physical appearance.

Other admirers couldn't take their minds off what the gems might be worth on the common market. In accordance with the travel rules, these would-be travelers were courteously ushered off the boat, as it made a brief stop before heading down the eastern river.

Earnest was sorry to see that happen and tried to make encouraging comments to those departing about their ability to recognize real value. But they weren't really listening. So, he just waved goodbye and saw even more clearly how important it is to have right motives when searching for the gold of prayer. Right motives are part of true alignment.

Now, Earnest could hear a few travelers contemplating another topic. What would it mean to be well connected to the Supreme Being? Earnest joined that discussion, for he too was a sincere seeker, and one who was soon to find out that the right connection was a spiritual necessity. The announcement was made that this next phase would require the willingness to reason things through.

That brought nods of agreement from the passengers, so the boat gently left the dock for the second lap of the journey.

* * * * * * * * * *

The first phase of our river journey was successful in that we found and uncovered buried treasure – *prayer*. Now a much larger work lies ahead of us as our boat expedition proceeds, having made a sharp turn onto the east river, the side of the Christ. It is this Christ, Truth, which brings us messages of good from God and enables us to communicate with our heavenly Parent. The Christ has a number of offices, such as the "spiritual idea of God," and the "spiritual idea of sonship." God is first and man as God's idea is second. Father before child.

On the city foursquare, the point of the Christ is "the spiritual idea of God." The star of the East, which shone over Bethlehem, lights our way to understanding the Christ, Truth. By following Jesus' path, this light becomes a floodlight shining a powerful beam on Jesus' life and earthly mission.

What Christ Jesus did for us

Christ Jesus paid a ransom, as the Bible puts it. But, he paid a ransom for what? Surely, it was for a spiritually-kidnapped world. He brought the world out of the darkness of that captivity when he demonstrated by his life that our connection to God is spiritual sonship, for he consistently referred to God as his Father and taught us all to pray to "Our Father, which art in heaven." It's a connection that can never be broken even by what appears to be death. We will rise above that experience, the change called death, and the grave too, with our connection to God still intact.

In a sense, Christ Jesus left the world a gold ring showing that connection—how spiritual man is wedded to God, his divine source. This ring, containing seven powerful petitions, was meant to be worn forever so we could pray to our Father. However, the Dark Ages descended and the value and meaning of the ring, the Lord's Prayer, were obscured. The world had to be reborn and reformed (the Renaissance and Reformation) to restore it to some degree.

We are still on that pathway today, to discover the value of the Lord's Prayer. *Science and Health* states on page 16, that this prayer "covers all human needs."

Now, it is one thing to return to the roots of prayer and realize that Mary Baker Eddy, in line with the Bible, maintained the asking, the requesting and the petitions of prayer, but it's quite another to really "unearth" this treasure and see it shine. Perhaps that's why her chapter *Prayer* in *Science and Health with Key to the Scriptures* contains that statement already quoted, "The world must grow to the spiritual understanding of prayer." (p.10)

One fact becomes very obvious as we look afresh at her chapter "Prayer"—it's all about asking. This is "the asking chapter" if we had to define it in one word, and mainly it cautions us how not to ask. The subject of sin is included, which makes good sense. Our prayer, a basic desire for genuine good, is the path that takes us to God, while sin, or wrongdoing, takes us off the track and away from God, away from everything that is truly good and lasting.

To whom are we praying? That's a good question. If we were stranded in a distant city, we would look for a familiar face, perhaps a good friend or dear relative to aid us. When my mother and I took the wrong train to Paris (my fault) and ended up in Amsterdam in the middle of the night, we made our way to my grandfather's home and knocked vigorously on the door until he awakened and let us in. That was a good solution and logical too, for we knew he would give us lodging.

Humanity increasingly knows God as divine Love through the Christ, Truth that comes to us moment by moment. It also becomes apparent that this Love is everywhere, surrounding us, caring for us and constantly providing all we need. We do indeed have the loving relative, who is unchangeable in love for us, who will always answer our knock on the door and freely give us what is needed.

Many years ago, I asked a woman what it would mean if she could only talk *about* her parents but never *with* them. Instantly she replied, "Well, that would be like death." That's how important it is to maintain the communication with our heavenly Parent. If we can talk with the GPS system in our car and receive an answer from a machine, we can certainly appeal to the intelligent power of the universe.

If divine Love, God, is truly alive to us then we can talk with God, ask questions regarding our welfare and how to bless others. In the 1960s some car bumper stickers proclaimed, "God is dead," only to be met by the facetious bumper-sticker retort, "My God is alive. Sorry about yours." A vital sense of God, who is Life itself, necessarily demands a communication *with* and an unbreakable connection *to* God. How to attain this wonderful state of connectedness, through the Christ, Truth and through prayer, will now be considered.

Desire, asking, deeds (D-A-D)

It's sweet to remember that Jesus addressed God as "Abba, Father" meaning "Daddy, Father." How tender and how connected! He always desired to do the will of God, and he announced that intention, prayed about it, and then he did it!

These three aspects are all there on the very first page of the chapter, "Prayer" in *Science and Health*. "Desire is prayer; and no loss can occur from trusting God with our desires, that they may be moulded and exalted before they take form in words and in deeds." So, we have desire developing into words and then taking form as deeds. Desire, words of asking, and deeds.

Perhaps we might think of it this way. Desire is like putting our TV on mute. Taking it off mute we hear the words of that desire. Watching the screen, we then see the actions that correspond with the words. Desire, asking, deeds. Each of these qualifies as prayer.

Some desires we'll simply toss away as worthless or selfish before even framing them with words. Other desires, such as for a good education, might take the form of words, and later deeds as the individual carries out that desire.

Let's recall the statement that ". . .waiting patiently on the Lord, we will leave our real desires to be rewarded by Him." (S&H 10)   What are our real desires?   Aren't they the ones that we are willing to put into action? We've all said things like, "Oh, if I could just go on a world cruise," but if the opportunity were to appear, we may not be eager to do that at all. No wonder we're counseled to trust God with our desires, so they can be reconfigured, if necessary, and cast in a new mold. We don't always know what we want, or even if what we want is worthwhile or good for us, so waiting and trusting God is the best course.

In *Science and Health* we find a definition of unceasing prayer. "The habitual struggle to be always good is unceasing prayer." (p. 4) It is also stated, "Consistent prayer is the desire to do right." (p. 9) The constant, wordless desire to be good is defined by Mary Baker Eddy as the way to follow the advice given by Paul to the Thessalonians, when he told them to "pray without ceasing."

It's an attitude one carries through daily life. Without that attitude or true desire, any verbal prayers we utter would simply be the "vain repetitions" that Jesus warned his disciples of before telling them how to pray. They are vain, which means worthless. Though they may sound good, there is no real desire to carry them out. "Praying for humility with whatever fervency of expression does not always mean a desire for it." (S&H 8) Again, we are faced with desire, asking, and deeds (D-A-D).

The Bible and the teachings of Christian Science give words to worthwhile desires that are taken to God. For instance, we have the Lord's Prayer with its spiritual sense, and in addition for church members there is the Daily Prayer and the admonition to pray daily and importunately on page 127 of *Miscellaneous Writings*. Even if prayed silently there are words attached to these desires.

Mary Baker Eddy actually provided the subject of prayer with what we might call a prequel and a sequel, not usually found in religion. She showed that prayer has its genesis in desire, which she also named prayer. Then the aftermath, or sequel to asking with great faith, is putting the prayer into the form of deeds. We are demanded to demonstrate or show our prayer. She even stated that, "The highest prayer is not one of faith merely; it is demonstration." And she goes on to say, "Such prayer heals sickness, and must destroy sin and death." (S&H 1) This is worth exploring more fully later on.

Let's return, for a moment, to the test of all prayer on page 9. On close inspection, we find that there is the desire, next the asking and then the doing, or living consistently with our prayer. All three are included in that test. The same pattern appears a number of times in the textbook, as on page 15, "Such prayer is answered in so far as we put our desires into practice."

In the past, it would appear that mainstream religion has accepted audible prayer that sounds right and good. The prequel, the prayer of desire, and the sequel, the prayer of demonstration, were not noticed or taken into account.

Today, this view is changing, and good deeds are expected, and even demanded, of humane humanity. This is evident on the national, political, local, and social scene.

The secret of effective petition

As with any secret, there is a discovery period. This will require the close attention of our group of seekers. We'll need to reason it all out together, that is, if we wish to arrive at the point of understanding petition and what really happened to it.

Now, we mentioned previously that Mary Baker Eddy did not discover prayer. Mankind had been praying for thousands of years, before she undertook her line of inquiry into the spiritual nature of things and searched for a healing system in the Bible. No, she did not discover prayer. What she discovered was a "metaphysical system of treating disease," based squarely on the Bible. In the process of this discovery, the subject of prayer was refined and elevated for all of Christendom. Even as Paul told the Athenians regarding God, "Whom therefore ye ignorantly worship, him declare I unto you" (Acts 17:23), so Mary Baker Eddy also declared the true nature of God. Gone was the punishing or corporeal concept of Deity, and in its place stood revealed an unvarying divine Principle, Love.

This understanding would become not only the basis for her system of treating disease but also a rock-solid basis for prayer. We could have complete faith in and turn to this heavenly Principle of life for answers, to find blessings for ourselves and others, just as we would turn in full faith to the principle of mathematics for numerical answers. So, enlightened faith took over from blind belief.

Here is the spot where it might be easy to simply gloss over the following statements, as they are rather well known. But by following them carefully and seeing how one thing leads to another, we will be rewarded. It's like pulling on a tangled piece of rope and seeing it straighten out. At this point, dear Colin Collector would simply head for his stash of books and articles to enlighten him, but we won't. We'll just stick with our textbooks. So, let's begin!

In speaking of the need for faith to advance to spiritual understanding, Mrs. Eddy wrote, "Faith, if it be mere belief, is as a pendulum swinging between nothing and something, having no fixity." (S&H 23) Prayer, based on blind belief, or half-hearted trust in the divine, is like that pendulum. It swings back and forth. Having no fixed Principle, it produces no fixed or certain results. Further explaining this point, in the chapter "Prayer" we find the following.

> "The prayer of faith shall save the sick," says the Scripture. What is this healing prayer? A mere request that God will heal the sick has no power to gain more of the divine presence than is always at hand. The beneficial effect of such prayer for the sick is on the human mind, making it act more powerfully on the body through a blind faith in God. This, however, is one belief casting out another, — a belief in the unknown casting out a belief in sickness. (S&H 12)

A belief casting out a belief is like, in Jesus' words, the blind leading the blind. They both fall into the ditch. Jesus prayed on a completely different basis and *Science and Health* illustrates the point that neither Science nor Truth acts through blind belief. Even the human understanding of the divine Principle does not act through blind belief, as explained on that same page.

It is neither Science nor Truth
which acts through blind belief, nor
is it the human understanding of the
divine healing Principle as manifested
in Jesus, whose humble prayers were
deep and conscientious protests of
Truth, — of man's likeness to God and
of man's unity with Truth and Love.

The above quotation is sometimes interpreted
to mean that Jesus' prayers were statements or
affirmations rather than petitions to God. A little
more detective work solves that one. Let's look at
what has been called "Jesus' farewell prayer" in
Luke 21. He begins his prayer with a request that
God would keep his disciples together, in unity, and
speaks of his own unity with God.

And now I am no more in the world,
but these are in the world, and I come to
thee. Holy Father, keep through thine
own name those whom thou hast given
me, that they may be one, as we are.

Jesus' prayer continues in this vein for a number
of verses, and then he widens the prayer.

Neither pray I for these alone, but
for them also which shall believe on me
through their word; That they all may

be one; as thou, Father, art in me, and I
in thee, that they also may be one in us:
that the world may believe that thou
hast sent me.

Here is where we find the "conscientious protests
of Truth" of which Mrs. Eddy wrote—the protests
of "man's likeness to God and of man's unity with
Truth and Love." These protests are still within the
framework of Jesus' prayer, of his requests to God for
the unity of his followers. He gave, as an example
of the unity he was requesting, his own unity with
God. Now, here is the important point. Jesus does
not abandon his communication with God by only
stating truth. His protests of Truth simply prove
that he understood the firm basis on which he was
asking God.

Jesus' farewell prayer is a perfect example of
the prayer that has the stabilizer of understanding,
rather than the instability of blind belief.

The reason he provides as to why he is asking
is not only trust and faith in God. He knew the
goodness of God, and had already demonstrated his
oneness with God.

This higher basis placed prayer in a completely
different light. Desire and petition were still there.
The Bible does not remove them, and Mrs. Eddy
never removed them. In following Jesus' example,
she scientifically explained the specifics of prayer,
which now had a firm basis. This new basis was the

acknowledgment, the understanding, that the good we are asking to see is actually already present. It has never been absent and never been lost. Why is that true? Surely, it is because of the nature of God, as the unvarying Principle of our lives. This understanding of God as divine Principle puts our prayer on a completely different track.

A large clue from the *Queen Mary*

A vivid illustration of this topic is not found on our boat, cruising down the prayer river, but on the Queen Mary as she ploughed across the Atlantic Ocean from Southampton to New York. Quite amazingly, I found myself, in my late teens, traveling in first class on her. That was quite a story in itself.

My dad was stationed in New York in the late 1950s working at the United Nations, and my mother was with him. I'd been living and working in London, when my parents sent me a ticket to join them.

It was for cabin class (second class) on the *Queen Mary*, though they really wished it could have been for first class.

When arranging for my trip at the travel agency in London, the agent told me that a ship had foundered off the English coast. In order to accommodate the extra travelers, some cabin class passengers would need to be moved up to first class at no extra charge. I'm sure you see where this is going. Yes, right in the direction of my parents' loving desire. As we chatted, the friendly young man said he would place me in a cabin all to myself. It would have its own bathroom, and be on the same deck as the Prime Minister's cabin. Would this do? Oh, yes, very nicely, I assured him.

That agent traveled on the same boat train from London to Southampton (a wild, rattling ride in an old train going about 90 miles an hour, or so it seemed). He even escorted me to my cabin. It was everything one could hope for. I noticed immediately there was a white telephone next to the bed saying calls could be made to anywhere in the world. That was a nice touch!

The journey on the *Queen Mary* was an adventure all on its own, and there were many items and events of interest that could be shared. For instance, the glass-ceilinged night club was unforgettable in that we literally danced underneath the stars.

However, it was only recently that another facet of the *Queen Mary* came strongly to mind. It's something that helps to explain so much of what really happened to prayer. And this too is a good example of how we receive the answers we need. They may take form in parable, allegory or analogy.

It was a rock n' roll era of music during the '50s, and that ship followed the beat. Yes, the *Queen Mary* was a rock and roll ship, rolling quite extremely from side to side. One might sit quietly in the main lounge listening to a string quartet playing beautiful, classical music, while the scenery shifted dramatically from an all-sky view one minute to all-ocean view the next, as the ship did her rock and roll dance. What could one say! You just got used to it. It was a year or so after I sailed on her that stabilizers were installed. No more rock n' roll for the *Queen Mary*!

Just as stabilizers were installed in the *Queen Mary*, the discovery of Christian Science installed a stabilizer into the worldwide field of prayer. The understanding and specific explanations of a constant, unvarying divine Principle meant that humanity can ask God, knowing that the good they desire is already there and waiting for them. Humble prayer shows how to access it. It's like going to the bank with the knowledge that the money is already in our account, not simply hoping the bank will take pity on us and give us what we need.

The Apostle James put it so beautifully in chapter 1:17, "Every good gift and every perfect gift is from above, and cometh down from the Father of lights, with whom is no variableness, neither shadow of turning." Let's think of what James is describing here. He speaks of every perfect gift, Father of lights, no variableness, no shadow of turning. What but a divine Principle could accomplish that!

Christendom so needed that stabilizer—the understanding that God is our divine Principle that never varies. Even the "holy, uplifting faith" which produced wonderful healing works in primitive

Christianity needed to have the firm basis of understanding. That basis was ushered in by Christ Jesus in a general sense but explained specifically in Christian Science, as on page 259 of *Science and Health*. "The Christlike understanding of scientific being and divine healing includes a perfect Principle and idea, — perfect God and perfect man, — as the basis of thought and demonstration."

Christian Science described and specifically installed a new basis for thinking and for demonstrating the Christ, Truth. This basis included prayer.

A striking instance of this may be found in the Lord's Prayer. "Thy kingdom come" is actually a petition, for the word *may* is understood. In giving the spiritual sense of this, *Science and Health* translates that into a statement of fact with, "Thy kingdom is come; Thou art ever-present." It had now been proved scientifically, through Christian Science and according to a divine Principle, that God's kingdom is indeed ever-present. This was the stabilizer that Christian Science had given to prayer.

The Lord's Prayer, usually uttered by a collective, needed to have that recognition. However, when adopting that same petition for the individual members of her church as their Daily Prayer, Mary Baker Eddy kept the line as a strong petition, which could not be simply stated but needed to be proved individually. There are actually five petitions in this prayer.

> "Thy kingdom come;" Let the reign
> of divine Life, Truth and Love be
> established in me and rule out of me
> all sin. And may Thy Word enrich the
> affections of all mankind, and govern
> them. (Manual 41)

It's interesting that this prayer, standing on the second point of the city foursquare, hearkens back to the Word of Life, Truth and Love, which is the first point of the city. It then looks forward to the next one of Christianity and all mankind. Evidently, it's not enough for church members to simply state that God's kingdom is present, though that is the basis of their prayers. They need to desire and prove it.

The Discoverer's great desire

It would be difficult to find, in any of Mary Baker Eddy's writings, a more emphatic statement as to when to pray, how to pray, what to pray for and its results, than that found on page 127 of her *Miscellaneous Writings*. In fact she spoke of this as her great desire.

> One thing I have greatly desired,
> and again earnestly request, namely,
> that Christian Scientists, here and
> elsewhere, pray daily for themselves;
> not verbally, nor on bended knee, but

mentally, meekly, and importunately. When a hungry heart petitions the divine Father Mother God for bread, it is not given a stone, — but more grace, obedience, and love. If this heart, humble and trustful, faithfully asks divine Love to feed it with the bread of heaven, health, holiness, it will be conformed to a fitness to receive the answer to its desire; then will flow into it the "river of His pleasure," the tributary of divine Love, and great growth in Christian Science will follow, —even that joy which finds one's own in another's good.

Her foregoing desire is the amplified version, we could say, of the petition in the Lord's Prayer, "Give us this day our daily bread," which is interpreted as "Give us grace for to-day, feed the famished affections."

Notice the manner of mentally petitioning, with hunger, meekness, importunity, humility and trust. Asking for bread, generally speaking, one receives "more grace, obedience, and love." Asking specifically for the "bread of heaven, health, holiness," the result will be "great progress in Christian Science" evidenced by joy for another's good. That's quite a distance to have spiritually traveled. But speaking of travel. . .

Whatever happened to prayer?

Earnest Eager found out early in his quest that prayer without a journey is really prayer without a purpose.

The *Queen Mary* was finally docked in Long Beach, California, where she is now a hotel and the host for many events. Glen and I stayed overnight in her many years ago, but it was a different ship from the one I'd known. Gone was the anticipation—the companionship and joy of the journey. The traveling music and laughter had fled the scene. It was difficult to recognize her.

Perhaps, what happened to prayer was something along those lines. It appears that, decades ago, when Christian Science was still relatively new on the world stage, the importance of the firm foundation, the stabilizer, captured attention. It was suggested that knowing the truth, which upheld the asking, was more scientific than the asking itself.

Why did this happen? Well, one can only imagine the joy of the Christians, the early Christian Scientists, who found their prayers equipped with a stabilizer. They loved the rock-solid truths they were declaring and knowing. It's even understandable why, with this new spiritually-scientific knowledge of God, and also with the ability to treat the sick, they asked the question: *Is it wrong to pray for the recovery of the sick?*

Reaffirming the need for prayer based on understanding, Mary Baker Eddy replied:

Not if we pray Scripturally, with the understanding that God *has* given all things to those who love Him. (Mis. 59)

Notwithstanding her statement, the joy over the stabilizer grew in favor until the understandable statements of truth, on which prayer was founded and which would have enabled prayer to travel safely, were given the name of prayer. That stabilizer was often termed a "prayer of affirmation."

Our prayer ship was virtually put into dry dock. For decades, petition was generally looked upon as infantile, outgrown and rather unscientific. Just as one could not possibly travel on the *Queen Mary's* stabilizers without the ship, so one could make no real progress without asking and following.

One can't sail or make real progress on prayer's stabilizers alone. It's impossible to state ourselves into the kingdom of heaven, into spiritual understanding. That's the goal and prayer allows for and facilities that spiritual journey.

The assumption could be made, and I must admit to having made it for some years, that we had lost prayer and needed to find it again. But it came to me while writing this book, that perhaps we never really totally had prayer to begin with.

In opting for the stabilizer, the statements of truth, students had indeed let go of the Christian asking, their petitions to God. They held tightly to the stabilizer as one would cling to a buoy in a rough sea. However, both parts were needed, the asking and the basis for it. Perhaps, in a way, we had not really lost prayer as *Science and Health* explains it. Maybe, we just hadn't quite "got it" yet. We were simply on the way to understanding what prayer really is. The actual need was to (1) have a firm basis for the request by understanding that good is always present, then (2) desiring and asking to see it, and (3) demonstrating it in our own lives and character. This is so different from treating a case in Christian Science.

Oh, the distinction between prayer and treatment appears quite clearly in the testimonies of healing both in *Science and Health* and in *Miscellaneous Writings*, where writers speak of Christian Science treatment. However, this distinction evidently didn't take strong enough hold to withstand the currents of thinking which favored *knowing* as prayer.

Added to that was possibly the desire of many early Christian Scientists to show that prayer in Christian Science was different from prayer in their former Christian churches. In a sense, a tenuous separation was accepted instead of a strong marriage of ideas. Whatever the reasons, it's a humbling subject, for it seems we constantly have to admit we are on the path to discovery and still have a distance to go. There are corrections to be made, and clarities to be attained all along the way. We can rejoice that progress is being made. Let's pause now to consider the idea of asking a divine Principle.

Praying to our Principle, divine Love

Mankind's view of God changed dramatically over centuries, as it transitioned from worship of celestial objects such as moon, sun and nature's wonders, to super-hero gods—those muscle men of great power. Today, those mighty heroes are only in comic books.

The Bible depicted God as a type of warlord needing to be appeased with human sacrifice, or who demanded the spoils of battle.

That aggressive view of God did, however, transition into the kindly shepherd of David's Psalms, a deity who was accorded more trust and reverence. That developing concept of God has to be one of the most valuable gifts of the Bible to mankind. It shows an ascending pathway of thought leading finally to the divine idea of God, who is Love. How may we describe Love that is God, which never changes and never errs? Only a divine Principle could really fill that description.

Religion is at a pivotal point again. Yes, mankind has come a long way, and there are signs of change still going on. There is a very large, well-known, non-denominational church only a mile from where I live, and many of my neighbors belong to it. I asked one such neighbor how he prayed to God. Did he pray to God as a person or as Spirit, as Jesus declared God to be? He replied, "I pray both ways, sometimes to God as a person and sometimes to the divine Spirit." It was an honest answer and probably indicative of where a good many of his fellow church members are in their view of the Supreme Being.

When Mary Baker Eddy was asked if she believed in a personal God, her answer evidenced her own transition to that higher view of Deity. She wrote:

"I believe in God as the Supreme Being. I know not what the person of omnipotence and omnipresence is, or what the infinite includes; therefore, I worship that of which I can conceive, first, as a loving Father and Mother; then, as thought ascends the scale of being to diviner consciousness, God becomes to me, as to the apostle who declared it, "God is Love," — divine Principle, — which I worship; and "after the manner of my fathers, so worship I God." (Mis. 96)

"Mother's Evening Prayer," a poem by Mrs. Eddy, showed her approach to God as the understood Principle of her life. She prayed to "O gentle presence," to "Thou Life divine" and "Thou Love." (Poems 4)

But people don't tend to feel close to a principle. An unexpected resource comes to our aid here. In our study of Christian Science, it's helpful to check a word as it appears *now* in the dictionary, and as it appeared *then*. The *then* is at the time the text was written. Mary Baker Eddy was well known for her thorough work with dictionary and thesaurus.

The first meaning of principle today is: "A comprehensive and fundamental law." In the 1800s the first definitions given were; "The cause, source or origin of anything, that from which a thing proceeds;".... "Being that produces anything." (*Student's Reference Dictionary*) How much closer we can feel to God as Principle with those earlier meanings in mind! Surely, most Christians would even agree with that as a definition for God.

Mrs. Eddy was obviously aware that this term might give us trouble, for she wrote:

> When the term divine Principle is used to signify Deity it may seem distant or cold, until better apprehended. This Principle is Mind, substance, Life, Truth, Love. When understood, Principle is found to be the only term that fully conveys the ideas of God, — one Mind, a perfect man, and divine Science. (No. 20)

God is not an unthinking principle such as contained in mathematics. As *Science and Health*, page 2, states: "God is intelligence."

How logical it is to pray, not to wood or stone idols, not to a finite person, but to the Supreme Being, the divine impersonal, impartial Principle, the intelligence, the divine Love, that is God.

A proof of mankind's search for a life principle is found in the oft-repeated statements that we are all learning life lessons. The concept implies that there is a principle with which we are conforming.

When speaking with a friend, a member of that large non-denominational church, she mentioned this idea. She was about to say that God was allowing for a problem, but suddenly changed her statement to declare that we are all learning life lessons. That was a huge leap—from a neglectful or unloving God to a classroom. I replied that if we are alert to those lessons, they tend to bring us closer to the truth of our being. She immediately said that was how she thought of it too.

It surely isn't too far-fetched to say the idea of God as the Principle of our lives is coming into view.

Divine Love communicates with us

If we can ask God, just how does God communicate with us? Love communicates in a heavenly manner with a divine message, the very one we need. "Christ is the true idea voicing good, the divine message from

God to men speaking to the human consciousness" (S&H 332). This message may appear "on earth" in many ways. We've heard accounts of people hearing an idea so strongly it seemed to be a voice. Others have related that the nudge to do something was so imperative they had to obey. The Christly message might be a Bible verse we turn to, or it could be a remark made to us. We may even see a billboard with instructions we need.

For instance, at one time I was praying about my next step when out walking, and a bus suddenly turned a corner in front of me. In huge letters across the side of the bus was written: "You're ready to write the next chapter." Shortly afterwards, I embarked on a new writing project.

No matter how clear the messages are, we find that the spiritual understanding of prayer still requires effort and practice. More digging on our treasure hunt is needed to totally unearth and inspect "this asking," as Mrs. Eddy terms prayer (S&H 9).

Why petition is answered

We have considered how petition should be on the stable basis of understanding. Yes, that is how it should be offered and with all humility, but why is petition answered?

On page 16 of her chapter, "Prayer," Mrs. Eddy speaks of "heaven-born aspiration" (aspiration is an ardent desire especially for that which is noble or spiritual). We are releasing "earth-born fear" to exchange it for "heaven-born aspiration." That is an obvious change of base, and "heaven-born aspiration" is our clue! What is born of heaven is recognized by heaven. That is, when unselfish, ardent desire is directed to our heavenly Parent—when it returns to the source from which it came—then it is recognized by God. God sees and witnesses His own idea returning to Him. He blesses it and calls it good.

Let's reason this through by using our textbook. To love one's neighbor as one's self is a divine idea, according to *Science and Health* page 88, so it does not emanate from a human being, and no one can lay claim to that idea. It belongs to divinity, to God. The word *idea* in Christian Science may be used in various ways, and the context will reveal its application. In some instances, the word denotes our idea of God, or it may point to God's idea or spiritual man. Or, as in the context above, *idea* may imply a divine plan by which something is carried out.

Loving one's neighbor as one's self is a concept or idea that the divine Mind, Love, has formulated as an integral part of the government for its own creation. When this idea or activity takes place on the human scene, divine Mind recognizes the idea as being its own. This recognition does not require the divine to stoop to the human level, because it is the idea itself, though employed humanly, that the divine recognizes. In the same way, we would recognize an idea that we had sent out, without knowing the details of how it was implemented or even the situation itself. Suppose we had come up with an idea of how to support the youth in our community. We wouldn't need to know the specifics or each instance in which the idea was employed or put to good use. The basic concept we had formulated would still be recognizable to us. We would say, "That was my idea!"

Though infinite, perfect Mind is not conscious of imperfection, human limitations or problems, yet the divine idea or activity is known to this Mind. It is at this recognition point that prayer is answered!

Let's think about this a little further. What God has sent out does not return empty, void or without fulfillment. "So shall my word be that goeth forth out of my mouth: it shall not return unto me void, but it shall accomplish that which I please, and it shall prosper in the thing whereto I sent it." (Isa. 55) Heaven-born aspiration is obviously from God, and it will prosper.

Heaven-born aspiration has no taint of earth, and so half-baked desires for someone's good are not acknowledged by the divine Mind, nor are selfish or doubting prayers. It is only as the idea returns to God in a pure form—the way in which it was sent out as heaven-born aspiration—that it is recognizable to God and therefore fruitful. The divine Mind is seeing, bearing witness to, what it has created and declaring it to be very good.

Jesus explained that witnessing: "And the Father himself, which hath sent me, hath borne witness of me." (John 5:37)

It is at this point, of God recognizing what He has sent forth, that the situation about which we are praying is resolved.

Asking better questions

Why can't I have the new car, the new job or even the new spouse that I'd like (and that I deserve, added under one's breath)? These are just a start on the wrong-question list. The options we face are usually limited by a human, incomplete view of life. It's the end-of-the-rainbow point of view, not a full-orbed promise of endless good. For instance, a young woman asking if she should marry Joe or Burt might have the wrong question, because she hasn't met Greg yet. Rather than zeroing in on the human need involved, she could ask for the joy in heaven, the companioning that's in the realm of harmony, to be made apparent on earth and in her life. Right here is a very important point and worth pausing for. That for which we ask has to be in heaven first, before we can ask to see it on earth. "As in heaven, so on earth." In other words, there has to be a spiritual fact behind what we ask for, or it isn't in heaven. And if it isn't in heaven, we may as well forget it!

Questions we ask our divine Principle are answered. They just may not be the answers we expect or for which we hope. They might be "Rephrase that question," or "No," or simply, "Wait!" Our desires will be "moulded and exalted," as the first page of the textbook declares. And the Bible calls wrong desires, "asking amiss." Asking for spiritual needs to be met always brings blessings. And for a very good reason. We have the opportunity to demonstrate our prayer.

Demonstrating our petitions

Demonstrate our petition? That's not usually how we think of the word *demonstration* is it? But if we always equate this word with healing or a certain good outcome, then we'll miss the spiritual understanding of prayer, and the following two statements won't make any sense. Here is where it's good to remember the stages of prayer; the desire, the asking, and the deeds.

"The highest prayer is not one of faith merely; it is demonstration" (S&H 16). We may think we know what that means until we read the next sentence, "Such prayer heals sickness, and must destroy sin and death." In this instance, demonstration couldn't mean healing because healing is the result of this demonstration. Surely the demonstration referred to means putting our desires into practice. "Self-forgetfulness, purity, and affection are constant prayers." (S&H 15) Having faith is a necessity, but living and demonstrating our prayer demands

79

more. We're told the deed is the highest form of prayer! This certainly enlarges our whole concept of demonstration as well as of prayer.

The term *demonstration* is often used as a type of euphemism suggesting we have obtained what we hope for, such as a new car (we got what we wanted). Well, we might demonstrate God's love in our lives and see the human need being met because of that demonstration, but we don't demonstrate material things, unless we are showing how they work. For instance, the person who demonstrates a car is probably a car salesman. We may even purchase a demonstrator car, as it's usually a good buy.

The most-needed prayer and the most-needed demonstration, according to *Science and Health,* page 3, is this: "What we most need is the prayer of fervent desire for growth in grace, expressed in patience, meekness, love and good deeds." That's under the paragraph heading of "Efficacious petitions."

Years ago, I shared a practitioner office in Los Angeles on Wilshire Boulevard. The building was tall and skinny, rather like a rocket. This may have prompted the elevator operator, when he found out what I did, to remark, "One more practitioner in here and the building will go straight up!"

Well, whether the building went up or not, I was determined to go higher spiritually. So, one day I was ardently praying for more humility. I don't know if I expected it to descend on me like a shower of heavenly moonbeams causing me to fairly glow with that good attribute, but I certainly wasn't expecting an immediate opportunity to demonstrate my prayer.

A man, whom I knew slightly, called and asked for Christian Science treatment adding, obviously tongue-in-cheek, "I would have asked this other person for help but she's out of town, so you're second best, but that's okay 'cause second best tries harder." I could laugh with him at his reference to a car rental commercial. How simple it would be if all our opportunities to practice what we ask for were as easy as that one! I didn't mind being second best at all, though at another time, his comment may have irked me.

Even if we truly desire something so worthwhile such as peace for our communities, or our world in general, the prayer for peace must be accompanied by the practice of peace in our own lives. That would be demonstrating our prayer. Whatever we pray for, we can be sure we'll be given the opportunity to put it into practice. All true prayer, as we've read, means we'll love our neighbor better than before, "better because of this asking." (S&H 9)

It's at this point, someone speaks up (and they always do) with a puzzling question. "Why are we supposed to pray importunately? Are we trying to change our divine Principle?" Good question, so let's consider it.

Asking importunately

The Gospel of Luke, chapter 11, records the Lord's Prayer. This is immediately followed by Jesus' strong statements about asking repeatedly and importunately, illustrated by a parable in which he described someone asking for three loaves of bread from a friend and being given them due to his importunity (urgent request). This may pose a little mystery to students of the Bible. We should ask with urgency? Why does Jesus say that?

Skipping entirely over these questions, the human mind comes up with the arguments, "We're not supposed to plead with God" or "We're not supposed to try to change God" and "God isn't a human we're trying to convince." And so forth and so on. Actually, human thought would rather dismiss this whole subject. Therefore to call it a mystery might be overstating, because one has to peruse a subject first, before it can be classified as a mystery.

Let's strongly resist the resistance to praying importunately and instead ponder why our Way-shower wants us to follow him in this direction. Just why did Christ Jesus want us to pray importunately, with urgency? He obviously knew that God "is in one mind, and who can turn him" (Job 23:13), so changing that Mind would be impossible. Is this knowledge in conflict with an importunate or an earnest, urgent petition? Not at all!

The urgency and frequency of the requests show the <u>petitioner's</u> sincere desire and eagerness, and have nothing to do with God's willingness to bless His dear children with the provision that is always at hand. What if that man had made a lukewarm request, received the bread and then just stored it away and not used it? How sincere is that! In other words, we really, truly have to yearn, ardently desire that for which we ask, intend to use it and then use it well. Desire, asking, doing!

In support of this concept, a woman I know sold her furnished home for a very reasonable price to family members. Then they proceeded to paint, give away, or sell off some of the beautiful furniture that had been so carefully collected for many years. Finally, the relatives suggested to her that she might like to buy the house back. She didn't! But the point is that their request didn't carry much weight or real desire in the first place. There was no great value placed on it, and as it turned out, they were not eager for very long to use what they had asked for. The doing, the appreciation of what they received was not present.

Rather than questioning God's love and abundance, it's far better to question our own willingness to listen to the Christ message, obey and receive the good God constantly has for us. The questions we can ask ourselves would then be: What value do I place on this? Will I use what He gives me? Will I actually follow His guidance?

When Glen passed on in 1993 there seemed to be a deep, black pit in front of me and the only way to avoid it was to pray with importunity. With pressing urgency, I asked, "Dear Father, what should I do?" I was feeling so lost this seemed to be the only viable request. Instantly I heard, as if spoken out loud, "Publish the book!" Those three words changed my life, and they changed the lives of many others also. I know this for a certainty, because I have a box of letters from all over the world to prove it.

The book was a manuscript my dad had been working on when he passed on fifteen years earlier, and it wasn't even finished. When asked about it, I'd make smug remarks such as, "Well, if it had meant to be published, it would have been." But now I was in a different mode altogether and desperately needed help. It also became clear that you don't argue with angels. So, I went to work and wrote a Preface and Epilogue, learned the computer, and set up my own company to publish it.

The Ultimate Freedom by John H. Wyndham, CSB came out in June of 1994, just nine months after Glen had passed, and the rest as they say "is history."

In four languages and on CD, this book is an ambassador introducing people all over the world to *Science and Health* and to a spiritual dimension many have only dreamed of. You might enjoy reading accounts of publishing this book, and the many surprising turns my life took afterwards.

Those details are in the book *Quiet Answers*. So, does importunate prayer work? Oh yes, definitely, yes!

No wonder Mrs. Eddy earnestly requests us to follow Jesus by praying importunately and daily for ourselves! Now, here is quite an amazing conclusion one can reach by following the reasoning of page 127 in *Miscellaneous Writings*. If we are not overjoyed at the good another receives, it's because we haven't prayed enough for ourselves! Perhaps it's like putting the oxygen mask on yourself first in the plane if necessary. That puts one in a good position to aid another. It is also akin to Mrs. Eddy's own prayer – "how to gather," "how to sow," then "how to feed Thy sheep." We learn to gather the understanding, how to plant the seeds, and how to feed others.

The result of asking importunately to be fed with the bread of heaven, of health and of holiness, is this: ". . . great growth in Christian Science will follow, – even that joy which finds its own in another's good." (Mis. 127)

At this point, it's not even necessary to work at being happy for others. One just can't help feeling that way. It simply bubbles over!

Now, we've been spending our unearthed gold of prayer on our own behalf for the sake of spiritual progress. And progress we must! It's the law of God, the law of good. The more we spend, the more we'll have for what waits round the next bend, which is the opportunity to help others.

Let's just emphasize an important point here. Prayer is what guides us, propels us, and shows the way. It is the process of proving humanly what we claim to be divinely true. Yes, it allows for the process of spiritualization of thought and life.

Insisting on simply declaring truths, without that process, we would expect the impossible—instant perfection from ourselves and everyone we know. What discontent that would breed! There is no instant perfection, for it a divine fact that needs to be proved step by step "As in heaven, so on earth."

This good instruction puts it in a nutshell: "Pray aright and demonstrate your prayer; sing in faith." (My 203) Singing really helps!

PART THREE

Traveling South: Christianity

Prayer for others and sacrifice too!

Earnest Eager was delighted beyond measure with the second part of his journey. He actually adored the concept of a divine Principle which is Love itself. The idea of a stabilizer to prayer intrigued him, and he was reassured about asking importunately, as that had always puzzled him. The Guidebook was becoming clearer to him now because of the Key book and the illustrations given on his quest. He wrote quickly in his notebook. There were so many gold nuggets to record from that last stage of the trip.

Another passenger had just passed by Earnest and given the news that the next part of the prayer journey would begin with how to comfort others. At that, Earnest was a little discomforted, even apprehensive. He doubted his ability to comfort. A few minutes later, there was more news, which was even more unsettling.

It was announced that the seekers might be asked to sacrifice something really important to them on the southern point. This caused a great deal of consternation. Did they really want to go there? After all, they had found the gold of prayer and how to spend it on themselves. Wouldn't that be sufficient? Couldn't they just skip the southern point?

Some passengers were wondering if they should simply leave the boat now, and it crossed Earnest's mind too. However, he knew it wouldn't fulfill the second road rule to love another as one's self. So he resisted the idea of disembarking and instead again set his face firmly towards the upcoming lessons.

A number of issues worried Earnest, especially the question about the place of religion and churches in today's world. Another passenger, who shared Earnest's concerns, reassured him by saying those very questions would come up at the south point. In fact, they may even catch sight of a golden butterfly, which would bring them much comfort. That news intrigued Earnest and other seekers too. It also quieted their concerns.

As the passengers became still and ready to listen and learn, the prayer boat set off and made the sharp turn onto the south river for the third stage of the expedition.

* * * * * * * * * *

The art of comforting

We've traveled the distance from finding the gold of prayer to the topic of spending it on ourselves. Of course, we would be eager to spend it on ourselves. Though the distance is the same, it seems to take much longer to reach the next bend of the river—to reach the point of helping others with our gold. It's a four-sided diamond as we recall, so each side is equally important, but it appears to take the human mind a lot longer to contemplate others' needs.

We're on the Christian side now and the demands are different. The Golden Rule, of doing unto others as we would have them do unto us, is now front and center. Someone asks if there are any provisions on our boat for this leg of the journey. Oh yes, we have a simple and rather underrated one, which is so potent it will feed everyone with just a few crumbs. It's appropriately labeled, "Comfort."

Let's dip into it and share some ideas on this subject as we glide along. *Science and Health* on page 234 states: "Whatever inspires with wisdom, Truth, or Love — be it song, sermon, or Science — blesses the human family with crumbs of comfort from Christ's table, feeding the hungry and giving living waters to the thirsty."

Our group is asked to take a few minutes to think of how just a kindly word or deed, a small crumb of comfort, has helped in their daily lives. It might have even changed their lives.

The phrase, "song, sermon or Science" reminds me of a story Ray Conniff told about a man who intended to commit suicide, but who heard one of a Ray's songs on his car radio and changed his mind. Not such a little crumb after all, was it! The effect was tremendous. Another one of his songs even brought a man out of a catatonic state. It's easy to imagine what a comfort that was!

A poem titled, "Signs of the Heart" was written by Mrs. Eddy in 1899, and in the first stanza she refers to a little heart. I read somewhere that a rubber band had fallen into the shape of a heart. She rejoiced in that small sign by writing, "O little heart, To me thou art, A sign that never can depart." And in the next stanza she took that hope higher. "O Love divine, This heart of Thine, Is all I need to comfort mine." (Poems 24)

Anyone, who has been comforted by a small sign, will know how she felt and how important it is to honor and rejoice over it.

Early one Sunday morning, I was feeling so alone in the work I was doing. It seemed that no crowds were vitally interested yet in exploring the difference between prayer and treatment. As I turned on the TV, I was saying to myself, "Oh, I feel so alone in this." Immediately, I heard a pastor preaching to his TV audience, "You are not alone. You are never alone." That was lovely to hear. Then I switched channels only to be faced with another pastor who was looking straight at me, it seemed, as he declared,

"You are not alone, and you never could be alone. That's impossible."

On that happy note, I decided to make breakfast. As I cracked an egg, a double yolk fell into the pan. That was such a plain message of comfort that it even made me laugh. Of course, it was impossible to be alone, as our heavenly Parent is always with us, giving instructions and ideas for His divine purpose. We'll have the right company on our journey by asking God to show us what is already present in that regard. Then it requires willingness and obedience to accept the answer, and the amount—even "being willing to work alone with God and for Him." (Mis. 118)

We are often unwittingly having a conversation with mortal, problem-filled thinking and become hypnotized by it. Looking away from a problem and turning our attention elsewhere is what a good thinker close to me refers to as "interrupting the conversation." Of course, something better and higher has to come next, but even the interruption can break the mesmerism. Humor can be a great mesmerism breaker. Yes, unexpected comfort and even healing can come from humor. You might recall the book by Norman Cousins, *Laughter is the Best Medicine*, which provided examples of that.

Here's my own example. I became quite frustrated, when learning a new computer program, which my dear techie expert Lynn, had installed. She insisted the new program was useful to my publishing efforts, but I said it was like having to learn to fly a 747 when all I wanted was a simple hang glider. She was not impressed with my logic, and so I pushed on until coming to a complete impasse. "I feel like the proverbial deer in the headlights," I protested. My helper didn't lecture me, or belittle my efforts. Instead she said, soothingly, "There's nothing out to get you. There's no car on the road coming at you, no bicycle, not even a cockroach on a skateboard!"

As you can imagine, we both burst into laughter at that mental picture, and the impasse bubble burst too. The learning of the program progressed and is still continuing. What took place? The danger or problem facing me was reduced in size to something meaningless, even ludicrous. What a tremendous help that was! It's something worth remembering and smiling about. There's nothing out to get any of us, not even a cockroach on a skateboard! Divine Love is truly in control.

How to comfort is not always easy to learn but so essential. We could even call it Healing 101. "If we would open their prison doors for the sick, we must first learn to bind up the broken-hearted" states *Science and Health* (366). One of the reasons Mary Baker Eddy gave for naming her discovery Christian Science was this: "I named it *Christian*, because it is compassionate, helpful, and spiritual." (Ret. 25)

Interestingly, she uses both *compassion* and *sympathy* in a positive way. The difference is that compassion, according to one dictionary, has the added quality of wanting to do something about the situation. It wants to relieve or solve it!

The discoverer of Christian Science wrote many poems but ended her slim historical volume *Retrospection and Introspection* with one by A. E. Hamilton that surely epitomized her life.

> Ask God to give thee skill
> In comfort's art:
> That thou may'st consecrated be
> And set apart
> Unto a life of sympathy.
> For heavy is the weight of ill
> In every heart;
> And comforters are needed much
> Of Christlike touch.

Let's add to that another poem, "Teach Me to Love" by Louise Knight Wheatley. It was republished in the *Anthology of Classic Articles* by The Christian Science Publishing Society in 2007.

From beginning to end this beautiful prayer reminds one of a statement by Mary Baker Eddy, "True prayer is not asking God for love; it is learning to love, and to include all mankind in one affection." (No. 39)

We may always ask God to teach us how to love and how to comfort. Let's never underestimate the power of comforting. It can save, and has saved, lives!

As we travel the south side of Christianity, we glimpse just how kind and loving true Christianity really is. Mrs. Eddy expressed the desire for all of Christendom to pray for the life of Love.

> I would that all the churches on earth
> could unite as brethren in one prayer:
> Father, teach us the life of Love.
>
> (My. 301)

It's that spirit of Love which meets human needs. "The letter of Science plentifully reaches humanity to-day, but its spirit comes only in small degrees." (S&H 113) That was written well over a century ago!

The human need

All through her writings, Mary Baker Eddy makes a clear distinction between the human and the divine. Nowhere is this more evident than in her statement, "Divine Love always has met and always will meet every human need." (S&H 494)

Another pause point here would be good. There are a number of references to "human need(s)" in our study books. It's patently obvious that we don't overlook the human need believing it is a super-fine metaphysical thing to do. Such activity would make us cold and uncompassionate. Divine Science without the compassion of Christianity is no longer true Science.

We can ask our heavenly Parent, to meet others' needs—to shed light on another's path—and we will receive an answer. But then an interesting query emerges. A young woman, on one of our prayer trips, said she didn't feel it was right to pray for a person with an obvious problem—someone she might see on the street. That would be like admitting the person had a need or lack in their lives. To her, that would be unscientific. Let's consider this.

Humanly there are needs. Divinely there is only supply, no lack. That's why divine Love is able to meet "every human need." By reflecting divine Love we play an active part, ". . .and blessed is that man who seeth his brother's need and supplieth it, seeking his own in another's good." (S&H 518) Our heavenward gaze doesn't overlook the human need. The old saying, "You can't be so heavenly minded, that you're no earthly good" rings true.

Here is what the Apostle James says about that in his Epistle, chapter 2, verse 15:

> If a brother or sister be naked, and destitute of daily food, And one of you say unto them, Depart in peace, be ye warmed and filled; notwithstanding ye give them not those things which are needful to the body; what doth it profit?

If we concentrate only on that demonstration of God's supply—the multiplication of the loaves and the fish—it's easy to overlook the fact that Jesus gave the perfect example of care for others' well-being. He wouldn't send the crowds away hungry after listening to his sermons, "lest they faint in the way." (Matthew 15:32) How utterly compassionate that was, as he took note of the human need. No cold assertion from Jesus!

It could be argued, as justification for lack of action, that he met that need through spiritual means. Until we can do likewise and spiritually multiply the supply needed, we shall obviously adopt the moral standpoint as we help meet the physical needs of others. Perhaps this is similar to the statement Mrs. Eddy makes about provision. She wrote:

> Till Christian Scientists give all their time to spiritual things, live without eating, and obtain their money from a fish's mouth, they must earn it in order to help mankind with it. (My 215)

Mary Baker Eddy earned her money by her writings and donated to local charities. She gave on that moral level of compassion. She was also aware of the most pressing human needs, which she met on the spiritual level. In answer to a newspaper item accusing her of being prayerless, she replied:

Three times a day, I retire to seek the divine blessing on the sick and sorrowing, with my face toward the Jerusalem of Love and Truth, in silent prayer to the Father which "seeth in secret," and with childlike confidence that He will reward "openly."(Mis.133)

Willingness to be alert to humanity's needs means we will be able to hear their calls for help.

Hearing calls for help

A Christian Science teacher, formerly an editor for the Christian Science periodicals, lived in Boston and was quite well known. During a visit with him, he told my dad and me the following story. One Sunday, he was sitting in The Mother Church listening to the service when the thought came to him, "Get up and leave." He said he smiled at that, knowing it had to be a devilish suggestion trying to get him out of the service. Once more it came, and again, he resisted. But when it came a third time and very forcefully, he got up and walked out. He realized that people might suspect he was in the throes of some kind of problem, but he obeyed anyway.

As he descended the church steps, he saw a car parked out front. A man was sitting inside peering up at the Church, so he asked the stranger if he could help him. The man replied he had always wondered

97

what that Church was about, but never felt he could go in. For the rest of the church service, our friend sat in that car and explained Christian Science to the stranger. He heard the call and answered it. We could conjecture it was a good thing only he heard it, otherwise there might have been a mass exodus from that edifice. But obviously, this was his work to do.

When the woman with "an issue of blood" touched the border of Jesus' garment in the crowd, he heard that mental call for aid. Likewise, Mrs. Eddy wrote, "From the interior of Africa to the utmost parts of the earth, the sick and the heavenly homesick or hungry hearts are calling on me for help, and I am helping them." (My. 147) We can also hear voices calling more plainly now, as we continue on our Christian river of thought.

The House of Light

Perhaps it's fair to assume, no matter what one's taste in art may be, that the paintings of Thomas Kinkade speak to us all. He painted houses with light streaming from the windows. Our House of Light has three porticos or main points. First is the power of right thinking and how it naturally blesses others. Secondly, prayer is directed to God regarding a situation or person. Thirdly, we are invited into another's mental home to aid them. That last is Christian Science treatment.

1. Light emanates naturally and effortlessly from the windows.

Light streaming through a window requires the obvious—a clean window!

An unforgettable cartoon of decades ago depicted a man sitting in his office, feet on the desk, simply staring out the window. He appeared to be doing absolutely nothing. The CEO, who was touring the business with the office manager, asked why the employee was permitted to do that. The office manager replied that the man was the idea person for the company. Immediately, the CEO ordered, "Then clean his window!"

The light issuing from a clear consciousness does heal. A man on a streetcar was healed due to the correct knowing of spiritual facts by the woman sitting opposite him. She was unaware of his need, but the light of the truth that she was dwelling on enveloped him. Mrs. Eddy explained it this way.

> The spiritual power of a scientific, right thought, without a direct effort, an audible or even a mental argument, has oftentimes healed inveterate diseases. (Rud. 9)

Surely that's what happened when that woman "with an issue of blood" touched the hem of Jesus' garment and was healed. It is recorded he felt that virtue went out of him. The light of Truth was so strong, as Jesus walked through their midst, that others were likewise healed. Jesus said of himself, "I am come a light into the world, that whosoever believeth on me should not abide in darkness." (John 12:46) How wonderful it would be to walk through life and have such an effect on others, that the light of the Christ, Truth, would dispel the darkness of fear, disease, sin and death.

Whether it is to bless the passerby or pray for another, or even give Christian Science treatment, the requirement of a clean window is still in effect. Yes, the windows of thought would necessarily have to be clear or transparent enough to let the light of Truth shine through. It's explained this way on page 295 in *Science and Health*, under the paragraph heading, "Goodness transparent."

The manifestation of God through mortals is as light passing through the window-pane. The light and the glass never mingle, but as matter, the glass is less opaque than the walls. The mortal mind through which Truth appears most vividly is that one which has lost much materiality — much error — in order to become a better transparency for Truth. Then, like a cloud melting into thin vapor, it no longer hides the sun.

With this in mind, the old housekeeper joke of, "I don't do windows" has no place in the vocabulary of sincere Christians. It's the most important task in our mental housecleaning efforts. My mother enjoyed telling about an ad for a housekeeper which she'd read in the LA times, "Has to be able to recognize dirt."

Someone on our prayer journey usually remarks that it's not scientific to look for dirt, and others will nod in agreement. Another voices the opinion that to look for or to see error in one's self is a negative activity. It's suggested that simply knowing ourselves as divine ideas is sufficient. Not so, according to the Bible and the teachings of Christian Science!

As *Science and Health* states, ". . .the human mind is the sinner, disinclined to self-correction." (218) Due to this we might assume that the petition "rule out of me all sin" (one of five in the Daily Prayer) is not a favorite of the human mind.

Jesus was not reluctant to point out and rebuke the errors in human thinking. He used strong words with the self-righteous Pharisees, as recorded in Matthew 23. He even called them hypocrites.

King David asked God in his Psalm 139 to search his heart, "And see if there be any wicked way in me, and lead me in the way everlasting."

Mary Baker Eddy agreed. Under the paragraph heading of "Searching the heart," she told us to examine ourselves to find out what we honestly are. (S&H 8)

She had even stronger words for it when she wrote of becoming acquainted with ourselves. (Ret. 86)

> Note well the falsity of this mortal self! Behold its vileness, and remember this poverty-stricken "stranger that is within thy gates." Cleanse every stain from this wanderer's soiled garments, wipe the dust from his feet and the tears from his eyes, that you may behold the real man, the fellow-saint of a holy household.

It's difficult to know, or put into practice, what is right, until we face what is wrong and correct it. A little more research into the term "self-knowledge" quickly sets us on a straight course. What is more, self-knowledge is the first of three steps to instantaneous healing. (Mis. 355)

Right motives help maintain a "clean window" and good transparency. Wrong or selfish motives muddy thought. In fact, "A wrong motive involves defeat." (S&H 446) That's a strong warning.

No wonder we're encouraged to question ourselves, including our own motives! For instance, why do we want to see more or better healing? The answer may be surprising and even unpalatable to us, in light of Mrs. Eddy statements about the true incentive (S&H 454) and why we lose our healing ability. (S&H 410)

Unceasing prayer helps keep our windows clean and so does praying actively each day to be filled with the light of Truth. Again, this isn't just for our own sake, but so the passerby may be blessed. It doesn't even require knowledge of the person receiving the blessing. It's a natural spiritual activity that has a natural outcome. However, there are times when one is quite conscious of another's need.

2. The occupant of the well-lit house goes to another's aid.

The occupant of the house sees someone stumbling in the dark across the street and so turns on the outside light to aid the traveler. That means we pray for the individual, who has crossed our path, as I did for the child in the Laundromat. To me this is similar to the following situation.

When my children were young, we lived across the street from their elementary school. The small parking lot on that side became the gathering place for older, rowdy teenagers, especially on weekend evenings. There was no proper lighting, so activities were carried on, cloaked by darkness. The next morning empty beer bottles and other unsavory items awaited the school children.

Something should be done to protect the school children and the teenagers too! But what could that answer be? After praying about it, the idea came to call City Hall and request lighting for that parking lot. They took the information down, but didn't give a hint as to what might happen.

Well, it wasn't too many days later that a very large truck, carrying a long pole light, arrived on the scene. My joy and gratitude, as I ran across the street to thank the driver, were surpassed by my surprise when he asked, "Where would you like it?" I picked the best spot, and there it was put! The wrong activity ceased immediately.

The government of our universe, our divine Principle, Love, is our City Hall, to which we may appeal in prayer. Here is an actual example of praying for another and the requests to give and take away.

A healing prayer

The Psalms are rich in petitions to God, as are many of the hymns in the *Christian Science Hymnal.* There are requests for God both to give and take away. "Create in me a clean heart, Oh God; and renew a right spirit within me." (Ps. 51:10) "Who can understand his errors? Cleanse thou me from secret faults." (Ps.19:12) "Give us vision clear, break earthbound fetters, sweep away the veil." (Hymn 66) "Take from us now the strain and stress." (Hymn 49) "Give me, O Lord, an understanding heart . . . And thus from sinful bondage be set free." (Hymn 69)

The Daily Prayer asks for both the giving and taking away. Let's allow for both when praying for others as well as for ourselves. They were both needed in the following healing.

It was in the fall of 2000 around eight on a Friday morning, when I received a call from my daughter at work. In hushed tones, she asked me to pray for the son of a woman in her office. Having been injured in a high school football game the night before, the boy had been rushed to the hospital and there given the diagnosis of a concussion and a broken neck. She told me the doctors were trying to assess just where they would go in to try and repair the damage, if they could.

My daughter didn't know the son or even his name but was very concerned for the mother and the situation she might be facing. Her compassion was deep and genuine, as that mother had already been through some hard experiences.

Prior to 1980, I would simply have cleared my own thinking by knowing that man in God's image could never be injured and other spiritual truths to that effect. But now I had gold to use—the well-tested gold of prayer.

It's not always necessary, I've found, to state the basis for our prayers. It may be well established in thought, and we can launch right into our petition with understanding and great faith. However, in this particular case, it came to me to establish those basics before praying.

First of all, I mentally reviewed the spiritual nature of man created in God's image and likeness. A spiritual idea cannot be broken or damaged in any way. There was no condition or situation that could deprive a child of God of his native inheritance of goodness and health. I was giving my prayer the stabilizer it needed.

Then, on that solid basis, I began my prayer and asked God to take away the fears surrounding that young man, including his own, his parents and those of the hospital staff. I asked for the sense of God's love to pervade his room and the hospital. I asked that the material laws in this situation be annulled and God's law be seen as supreme and that the physical evidence of injury be removed. I asked that no counter influence might prevail, but that he could recognize his God-given freedom and harmony.

These requests were not only for harmony to be given the boy but for anything opposed to that harmony to be taken away. My petitions finally ended with something unusual for me. I found myself asking for this healing in the name of the Father, the Son, and the Holy Ghost, as I understood them in Christian Science, ending with, "Thank You, Father!"

You may notice that the petitions were all addressed to God and no arguments were made on the boy's behalf. Then I released it until about eleven that morning, when the thought came I should pray again. Immediately I heard mentally, "Don't! It's already done!" So I didn't. Later that evening I heard what happened. Prior to the operation, which was scheduled for 4 p.m., more tests were taken. These tests showed no concussion and no broken neck! There being no reason to keep him longer, the boy was discharged at about the same time as the operation had been scheduled.

He went home that Friday evening and back to school on Monday. I am convinced it was my daughter's compassion that paved the way for the prayers and that healing.

My daughter did tell her co-worker about the prayers for the boy. When he was healed, the mother then e-mailed my daughter, both rejoicing and puzzling over it. She wondered if it could have been the prayers that did it.

A few years later, when I saw the boy's mother again, she told me of her son's high school graduation, then looked at me earnestly and said, "I don't think I ever thanked you properly." But it wasn't until even later, in 2008, that the details actually came out. At that time, she gave permission to write up what she told me. These are her words in e-mails. It was now eight years since the incident on the football field.

> Yes, he definitely did suffer a concussion. He didn't know what year it was, who the president was and stuff like that. He was disoriented and that is why he was taken to the hospital.

Once at the hospital, the initial x-ray of his head showed a break and that was when he was immediately put into a neck brace and completely immobilized. I stayed the night with him at the hospital and watched the tears stream down his face. He was not in pain...he was afraid of being paralyzed.

It was really weird when the doctor finally came to the hospital room to discuss everything. He had Michael move this, move that, touch your nose, all kinds of things and then all of a sudden he said, "take off that neck brace, you don't need that." We were all shocked, what the h... was he talking about, and that's when he said, "he's fine, take him home." Too, too weird, that's why we had to get a second opinion. It all wasn't making any sense to us.

She wrote that she and his dad took him to another neurosurgeon for a second opinion. They expected him to say that the neck was not broken and never had been, but that's not what they heard.

The second opinion surgeon ordered a very definitive, specialized test that would for sure show if there was a break or not. The test came back...yes...there is a break which would explain the numbness and tingling he was having in his arm and fingers. But that this was the extent of the result of a broken neck was a MYSTERY. I remember the way he looked at us when he told us. It was not a look you would expect to be on a doctor's face. I do believe his MYSTERY was our miracle. I thank you God and will be forever grateful.

The mother related that the numbness and tingling were soon gone, and there were no further repercussions. The boy even went to college on a baseball scholarship.

We may certainly ask that error, sin, disease or sickness be ruled out of our own or another's experience. This prayer, addressed to God, is not an argument for a patient, nor is it intended to rearrange someone's thinking. It goes to God and is left with God. But the prayer must be without doubt and full of faith in God's goodness and constant care. There can be "no opposing element." The prayers of a nation even have to meet that standard.

When Mrs. Eddy was asked why President McKinley didn't recover from a gunshot wound, despite all the prayers uttered on his behalf, she gave this reply.

> Had prayer so fervently offered
> possessed no opposing element, and
> President McKinley's recovery been
> regarded as wholly contingent on
> the power of God, —on the power of
> divine Love to overrule the purposes
> of hate and the law of Spirit to control
> matter,—the result would have been
> scientific, and the patient would have
> recovered. (My. 293)

Yes, we may pray for individuals or for the collective. "Prayer for Country and Church" pages 14 and 15 in *Christian Science versus Pantheism,* urges us to *pray* for our country's government—to pray for our Chief Magistrate, Congress and for our military. This is in line with Paul's exhortation to Timothy that prayers be made "for all that are in authority; that we may lead a quiet and peaceable life in all godliness and honesty." (1 Tim. 2:2)

Sometimes, those who are not yet making a distinction between prayer and treatment will endeavor to make sure they are not intruding by praying for "the office of the president." However, Mrs. Eddy is specific in the prayers she asks of us. If we are praying to God and leaving that request with Him, there is no intrusion. So, we may importunately pray, "Dear Father, may Your presence guide and bless our chief magistrate ..." (Pan. 14) The prayers for congress and our military are on the same lines.

There are examples of praying about acts of terrorism in *Quiet Answers*, so I won't attempt to duplicate them here, but just briefly, we may circulate a petition though our collective prayers to the Supreme Being that those false subjects of hatred and terrorism be removed from our earthly school, its catalogue and classrooms. May no one be misled to sign up for such a class. May it be canceled not only due to low enrollment, but especially because it does not appear as a subject in heaven. "As in heaven, so on earth."

3. The neighbor next door invites you in.

A neighbor asks for help on a certain problem he has in his own house. There is a dark spot giving him trouble and he can't figure it out. The occupant of the House of Light may have formerly prayed for his neighbor. But, being invited to enter the house, he may now give him Christian Science treatment.

Being invited to look into someone's mentality is the only correct pathway to giving Christian Science treatment. We do not enter a person's mental home without that invitation. (See "Obtrusive Mental Healing," Mis. 282) However, the individual is asking for more than treatment, which is only a means to an end. He is actually requesting Christian Science Mind-healing, in which the divine Mind, God, is the healer and the system is entirely spiritual.

Mary Baker Eddy set up and gained a state charter for her Metaphysical College, where her "metaphysical system of treating disease" would be taught. One can trace, through her writings, the references to this system of Christian Science Mind-healing. We'll take just one such statement, which provides an overview of the subject.

> Christian Science Mind-healing can only be gained by working from a purely Christian standpoint. Then it heals the sick and exalts the race. The essence of this Science is right thinking and right acting — leading us to see spirituality and to be spiritual, to understand and to demonstrate God. (No. 12)

Christian Science treatment is employed for Christian Science Mind-healing and it is a generic rather than a specific term, just as medical treatment is a generic heading for a kind of treatment. The specifics have to be explained in both cases.

Christian Science treatment is the application of the truths of God and man to a case needing healing. The appearance of disease is not part of God's perfect creation, where He saw everything and it was good. It is a false belief of the human mind and not a divine fact. The divine facts are aimed at refuting that falsity. The patient's state of thought is also taken into account and his fears are allayed.

The chapter "Christian Science Practice" shows there are two ways of taking on a case. You either have the case thrown out of court, or you go in and argue it. Here's how that plays out.

A lawyer might be so in tune with the laws of the land that he knows instantly that a case should be, and will be, thrown out of court (no real substantiating evidence at hand to prosecute it, for instance). Just so, a Christian Science practitioner could do likewise by being so clear on the true spiritual laws and facts that he doesn't need to argue the case for a patient. That would mean instantaneous healing, and it's described this way: "If Spirit or the power of divine Love bear witness to the truth, this is the ultimatum, the scientific way, and the healing is instantaneous." (S&H 411)

A math whiz, who is in tune with math, could instantly know the answer to a problem, while the rest of us might have to take the time to work it out by using, or going through, the rules. *Miscellaneous Writings*, page 352 explains these two options.

> Through the divine energies alone one must either get out of himself and into God so far that his consciousness is the reflection of the divine, or he must, through argument and the human consciousness of both evil and good, overcome evil.

If the healing is not instantaneous and if the practitioner needs "arguments of truth for reminders" then that more lengthy process must be adhered to. More precisely, "...you continue the mental argument in the practice of Christian healing until you can cure without it instantaneously, and through Spirit alone." (Mis. 359) It takes humility to be willing to argue the case.

The following experience is included, because it contains an example of how prayer may be used in conjunction with Christian Science treatment.

Early on in my practice, I was asked to treat a young teenager for a very severe painful physical problem. The healing was not instantaneous, so I proceeded with truthful arguments to win that case, and the freedom of the patient.

However, after a couple of days of arguing the case scientifically and metaphysically, there was no change. I have to admit it was with some concern, I reached out to God importunately, "I would do anything to see this healing."

Immediately, as if spoken out loud, I heard the words, "Even forgive.........." That was strange, because I'd already forgiven that individual, who had caused my family much discomfit and sorrow by their actions. Why, I had even gone so far as to meet with the person on a very kind basis. Then, Jesus' example came to mind, and it occurred to me that I'd only forgiven the individual, but not the situation itself. Oh, there was a big difference!

Quite suddenly, I saw that the forgiveness of the crucifixion is when we forgive the person involved, or those who have harmed us. But the forgiveness of the resurrection is when we forgive the situation and rise above the whole event, so that it becomes a non-event in our lives. (This will be discussed again in a moment.) That day, I was able to forgive the situation, and that same day the girl was healed.

Interestingly, the mother later told me that her daughter had been unforgiving towards a relative. The idea of forgiveness was exactly what was needed for her case and for my own as well.

My reaching out to God in prayer brought an immediate answer that helped win that court case for the patient. It was as though a special message had been delivered to the lawyer in court with instructions that he himself needed to obey. The lawyer paused to read and implement the message and then continued on with arguing the case.

Under the heading, "The Way" and in the first section to do with self-knowledge, is the explanation of what happened here.

"Cast the beam out of thine own eye." Learn what in thine own mentality is unlike "the anointed," and cast it out; then thou wilt discern the error in thy patient's mind that makes his body sick, and remove it, and rest like the dove from the deluge. (Mis. 355)

The point of Christianity

We've traveled the side and are now at the point of Christianity. Thus far we've seen how important caring and compassion are, for they belong to true Christianity. We've found we can meet someone's need through prayer, and seen the difference between that prayer and Christian Science treatment. Now, here is a more demanding aspect, and the Southern Cross shines an unwavering light on it. Let's weigh anchor at this southern tip. There will be no disembarking, for this is the point of no return.

It is strongly recommended that you now take a break in your reading. The foregoing uncovering of prayer for others is of such value that it would be a shame to eclipse it. I even wondered whether to include the upcoming discussions, but they are a vital part of Christianity—the very point of it. Our individual and collective praying of "Not my will, but Thine be done" will undergo strong testing. Will we "love our neighbor better because of this asking?" Will we be able to rise to the occasion in extreme or life-changing situations? That is our opportunity.

The lessons of the Southern Cross

There are two very large issues that face humanity, and they are common to most of us. One is the necessity for forgiveness, and the other can only be described as the "letting-go" lesson, where we sacrifice or give up some of our dearest hopes and aims. If we don't pass the forgiveness and letting-go tests, it's almost impossible to continue with the journey. So, let us now deal with these two subjects—our hurts and our hopes.

First of all, it's useful to classify our hurts which can sometimes be imagined or exaggerated. In terms of baseball, we need to know if we're playing in the minor or major league of hurts. The frequent annoyances, arising through differences of likes, character or opinion, are definitely in the minor-league category. If we don't want to strike out when dealing with them, it would be wise of us to heed the counsel contained in "Taking Offense" to "go forth into life with the smallest expectations, but the largest patience..." (Mis. 224)

That whole paragraph is the perfect remedy for minor-league annoyances and their almost constant disappointments. It gives instructions on reaching first base and demonstrating the Christ character. Going much farther than the good advice of "don't sweat the small stuff," which refuses to react, this vigorous play in the game of life starts us round the bases. It instructs us to act and come up to bat with patience, appreciation for good, genial temper, equanimity and a charity that is broad and sweet.

The human mind, as we can't help noticing, is inclined to place large expectations on people, but rather small ones on God. Let's reverse that if we'd like to make a home run!

The importance of forgiveness

Now, we turn from the minor to the major leagues, where there is much to forgive and forget. Here is the cardinal point of Christianity.

So much is demanded of us to live up to that title of Christian. It means both willingness to meet the human need, as God dictates, and arriving at the point where we will leave behind, or sacrifice, what divine wisdom mandates.

The Christianity point on the city is described as the "outcome of the divine Principle of the Christ-idea in Christian history." (S&H 577) One very decided outcome was the event of the crucifixion and what it did for the world.

Just how important is the cross to our history? Mary Baker Eddy wrote that "The cross is the central emblem of human history." (Un. 57) Where would we be without it? "Without the cross and healing, Christianity has no central emblem, no history." (Mis. 357) The Southern Cross spells sacrifice to human thought for it represents "the Cross of Calvary, which binds human society into solemn union." What may our own lessons be at this cardinal point? The Southern Cross will shine its light on our question and the answer.

Forgiveness is one of the most difficult lessons to learn on the human scene. One reason is that so often we just don't want to forgive, because harboring hurt feelings seems quite justified. Attributed to many authors, and fine thinkers, is the concept that hatred, resentment, or unforgiveness "is like drinking poison and expecting the other person to die." Even the unwillingness to forgive is a form of hatred, either of the person who committed the wrong, or else of the situation itself.

Naturally, we are not required to condone evil but to see through its seeming reality, and that takes some doing, doesn't it! But, that's exactly what Jesus did on the cross when he prayed to God, "Father, forgive them; for they know not what they do." (Luke 23:34) Jesus even felt compassion for his persecutors, those who were attempting to kill him. They didn't know what they were doing to the best man that ever walked the earth. They didn't know the truth of their own being, that would never countenance such an act of atrocity. They just didn't know! That blindness to goodness was using them, and Jesus understood that. And yes, he had compassion for their moral and spiritual blindness as much as he did for those who were physically blind, whom he healed. He prayed for them, just as Mrs. Eddy did for her enemies, and as we must too.

He wasn't overlooking the act or the evil portrayed in it, but he did have compassion for the unwitting dupes of evil, who were under that false influence. It will take Christly compassion on our part to follow Jesus and forgive those who commit sinful acts against us. In her beautiful Message to her Church in 1902, page 18, Mary Baker Eddy wrote:

> The Christian Scientist cherishes no resentment; he knows that that would harm him more than all the malice of his foes. Brethren, even as Jesus forgave, forgive thou. I say it with joy, — no person can commit an offense against me that I cannot forgive.

Immediately preceding that statement, she spoke of how Jesus had hastened to comfort his unfaithful disciples after his resurrection.

In expressing that compassion, Jesus gave us an example of forgiveness and love. That was not all, for there was more. He gave another and higher example, when he met two of his followers on the road to Emmaus. They didn't recognize him or the fact that he had risen above that experience, for they were lost in grief as they talked about that awful event. So, when Jesus asked them, "What things?" were they speaking of, they thought he was a stranger and just hadn't heard. After he explained why he'd had to go through the crucifixion, they finally recognized him.

Obviously, Jesus hadn't humanly forgotten, but he had divinely expunged that event as being meaningful. He had even forgiven the experience itself! It didn't exist and couldn't have taken place in divine reality, and that was his standpoint of thought, the basis from which he lived and healed. There was neither a persecutor nor a persecution.

Surely, if Jesus had not forgiven the perpetrators and the savage act as well, he could not have risen above it all and left the tomb. He truly hit a heavenly home run. In his ascension, he reached home, that state of real being, and the Christ, which was his spiritual nature.

The forgiveness of the crucifixion and the forgiveness of the resurrection, and the difference between the two, was not only a watershed of enlightenment for me in the healing of the teenager, but it has been of almost daily help on the journey. It is often far easier to forgive the individual, especially if one cares about them, but the situation is more difficult. That's why we sorrow over a sad movie. We know the hero, the actor, isn't really dead. It's the situation which disturbs us and gives us grief, especially if we identify with it. This understanding of the two types of forgiveness is certainly a great lesson and a tremendous help.

The other lesson under the Southern Cross is likewise a vital one, and we'll consider it now.

The obedience lesson: Letting go

Obedience to God's law isn't always easy to achieve on the human scene. It seems to require so much and usually in the sacrifice or letting-go department. "Not my will, but Thine be done" is the centerpiece of forgiveness and of letting go, for we have our own human will to contend with.

John the Baptist knew that he had to decrease so that the Christ, Truth, which Jesus demonstrated might increase and take center stage. Jesus knew he had to go away or the Comforter wouldn't come. Oh, there would be the temptation to hold on, at least by those who were followers of John or Jesus, but that was not the way to go. It truly was not "in the stars"—the Southern Cross. Each time there was a letting go, it was not an end, but simply a new beginning. Undoubtedly, this history will repeat itself for us.

The southern point is where we give up our human will and false desires, and that is why many have no wish to arrive at that point at all. "Not my will, but Thine be done" is a tough petition to pray and really mean. Consider Peter's declaration that Jesus should not have to go through the crucifixion, and how Jesus rebuked him with, "Get thee behind me, Satan: for thou savourest not the things that be of God, but the things that be of men." (Mark 8:33) Peter was so reluctant to follow Jesus to the southern point of the city that he even denied him three times! He was one who would gladly have cut across from the east to the west points on the diamond, thus bypassing the south altogether. But then history would have been robbed of its central emblem—the cross.

When it was time for Jesus to go on the cross, where was the safest place he could be? That was the question Glen and I asked ourselves and others.

The answer was obvious. The safest place for Jesus was on the cross, because it was the most obedient. The reward was great, for it put Jesus on the path to ascension, but not through death, though it seemed to be. It was the living, vital pathway of obedience to the Christ, Truth. He was at the pivotal point of Christianity.

Christ Jesus had to relinquish his own (very understandable) human desire to forgo the crucifixion. It's recounted in Matthew 26 that he actually prayed importunately three times (he even fell on his face as he prayed) to have that cup, that experience, taken from him. Then each time he also prayed and reaffirmed his willingness to have God's will be done. It was recorded that his sweat "was as it were great drops of blood falling to the ground." (Luke 22:44)

Being born of a human mother, but representing the divinity of the Christ, Jesus had two elements to deal with. The challenge was that "the human concept antagonizes the divine." (Mis. 309)

> When the human element in him struggled with the divine, our great Teacher said: "Not my will, but Thine, be done!"— that is, Let not the flesh, but the Spirit, be represented in me." (S&H 33)

That same chapter also asks and answers the obvious question. "Was it just for Jesus to suffer? No; but it was inevitable, for not otherwise could he show us the way and the power of Truth." (S&H 40)

Surely, what we, individually and collectively, are required to let go of has to pale in light of Jesus' demonstration of obedience.

Many were the instances in which Glen and I would consider how to become more obedient. Some were easier than others. It was a subject never far from our thoughts and hearts. Interestingly, we found that usually the more difficult was the obedience, the greater were the rewards.

Example #1

Letting go: An individual experience

One experience I had of letting go was after I had published *The Ultimate Freedom*. The book was met with instant joy and great receptivity by so many religions, and literally flew off the printing press into eager hands waiting for it all around the world. It traveled, by word of mouth, to little known and exotic places like Kuala Lumpur in Malaysia and islands such as those of Hawaii and the Seychelles off the coast of Africa.

Letters of gratitude poured in too! That small book helped introduce seekers and thinkers to Christian Science and reassured those who were already on that path. But then a large question arose in my mind. Wasn't I now in a different profession other than my advertised one of Christian Science practitioner? Yes, I was wearing another hat too, that of publisher and everything that went with that busy occupation. My constant desire, my prayer to be obedient was about to be put to a large test.

It became obvious that I was holding three books, and I had to let one of them go, just out of obedience. First was the *Church Manual* with the stipulation that one doesn't advertise their full-time practice of Christian Science in *The Christian Science Journal*, if they are employed in another profession (unless an official one).

The second was the *Journal* in which my advertisement appeared, and then there was *The Ultimate Freedom*. Yes, obviously I had to let go of one of these, but which one? Well, I couldn't let go of the *Manual*, and I couldn't let go of the mandate to "publish the book," so I released the *Journal* by removing my advertisement.

Just to give you a clearer view of the enormity of this decision, I'll recount a little of my background. My practice began in 1961, a few years after Sunday School, and I became *Journal* listed in the latter sixties. Over the years, I'd given numerous talks to churches and groups, plus association addresses, and written for the Christian Science periodicals.

The sudden omission of my name could be noticed, and it was! Literally overnight, it seemed, my reputation as a solid and faithful Christian Scientist was questioned, along with my new profession. The income from my practice likewise was affected. Though some activities, such as taking cases in the practice and giving addresses, continued for a time afterwards, still so much of what I had been totally immersed in for so long seemed swept away, taking income and reputation with it.

We won't travel further into the specifics of that period, but perhaps they can be summed up by two small instances. Early on, a woman sent me a letter chiding me for publishing something on Christian Science, for she felt that was the province alone of the Christian Science Publishing Society. My reply was gentle, as I pointed out the *Manual* By-Law on "No Incorrect Literature," which obviously allowed for other publishers. She then expressed gratitude for my kind answer and even sent me a fifty-dollar check to help with the work.

At another time, I was speaking to an individual, who worked at The Mother Church. She spoke so highly of *The Ultimate Freedom*. When I commented that I had given up everything to do that work, including my *Journal* listing, she emphatically replied, "You did the right thing!"

She knew, as did I, that the worldwide effect of the book was so much greater than anything my own individual practice could possibly accomplish at that point. As time went on and the book gained in recognition, my motives and work were no longer so often in question. In fact, the subject rarely comes up anymore. As for the income, well, divine Love has always supplied my needs during these years, and I've been willing to take steps in accord with divine wisdom.

Just the benefit *The Ultimate Freedom* has been to those in prisons in this country, in Ireland, and in Puerto Rico, would be enough to justify its presence. But it has done so much more, and instances of healing have been recounted in articles and testimonies appearing in the Christian Science periodicals, and in church meetings.

A friend told me, as recently as 2015, that at one Wednesday night testimonial meeting in her branch church, someone had started off with gratitude for that book, and then four or five more testimonies on the same subject followed. Yes, the book was doing much more than ambassadorial work. It was giving hope and reassurance to so many.

A deep desire fulfilled

There was no way I could have imagined what my life would be like after publishing *The Ultimate Freedom*. For instance, the new path even included writing and composing two metaphysical musicals, an endeavor for which I'd had neither desire nor training, unless you count a lackluster period of about two years learning the piano in my youth. Two of the songs from one musical have been sung as church solos and one of them in The Mother Church. I'm only including this information to show that what we are able to do under God's plan is something that none of us can second guess, visualize, or outline.

My life had been devoted to Christian Science both in the practice and in my church work. It never occurred to me that any change would come or be justified. It was usual for students to enter the practice after a career and not the other way round. A dedicated worker, in an official capacity, even wondered what kind of a message that would send to the Field. I wanted to say I hoped it would send the message of obedience, and that we can't always determine how obedience looks.

However, a new recognition recently surfaced that more than obedience was at work in this situation. For so long, in the deepest parts of my being, dwelt the great desire to share Christian Science with the world, in order to join with Mrs. Eddy's life purpose—to "impress humanity with the genuine recognition of practical, operative Christian Science." (Mis. 206) And I was willing to do this by any means at my disposal. That desire was fulfilled through publishing *The Ultimate Freedom*.

We find this statement about our careers in the book, *Unity of Good* on page 3, where Mrs. Eddy tells of God's guidance. "He has mercy upon us, and guides every event of our careers. He is near to them who adore Him." Glen would say to those questioning their life or career, "It's none of your business!" He was right. Our lives, our careers, are not ours but God's business, and we can yield to that unerring guidance, though it may appear contrary to human opinions or customs.

The beautiful song, "How We Imagined It" by Dawn-Marie Cornett, which was posted on YouTube by TMCYouthChannel in December of 2013, tells how the birth of Jesus came in a manner that was totally unexpected, even humanly questionable. And yet, it was so right! That was exactly the way it should be.

https://www.youtube.com/watch?v=8AVpz_b6AXI

Example # 2

Letting go: A collective experience

That song could be the theme song for this era. It certainly is not how we imagined it would be, as so many Christian churches dwindle and close all over this country, and in other countries too. A new era had taken hold, and what a challenge that was and is to the religious establishment!

The very popular British TV series *Downton Abbey* was a stark portrayal of the uneasy and even reluctant transition into a new era. There were many pithy sayings usually uttered by the Dowager Countess, played to perfection by Maggie Smith. I believe it was she, who remarked that it was better to evolve than become extinct. During the dismantling and selling of one fine old estate, including the couple's wedding gifts, the titled manor owner complained they had hung on for too long, until there was nothing left.

Perhaps the last lines of the final episode were the most telling, when Isobel remarked, at New Year's Eve, that they were toasting the future. "We're going forward into the future, not back into the past," to which the Dowager Countess dryly replied, "If only we had the choice!"

It's as though the change in era, which had been underway for some time, had suddenly caught up with them and taken them by surprise.

Many in the religious field feel the same way today as the symbols of religiosity—churches and affiliated institutions—are waning. Oh, to return to the glory days of religion with people flocking to the local church on Sunday! (Not to mention the Sunday dinner after church, which was often a family occasion, as it was during my youth in Sydney.) But that era isn't returning.

Glen and I sensed these winds of change, and it was early in the '80s when we remarked to a nurse that her medical field would soon be surpassed by the scientific one. She immediately replied, "It's already happening!" The prayerful investigation we pursued on the eras finally led to a book written as a novel in 2014, titled: *Three Gifts: the Eras of Science, Medicine, Religion.* Where religion has been, and where it is going, is explored in that writing.

It is no longer the religious era of Mrs. Eddy's day, and one cannot approach things in the same manner. For instance, it's useless to insist on attracting more buyers to our horse and buggy business, when everyone else is driving an automobile. Even dedicated prayer could not accomplish that feat!

The religious era of *Downton Abbey* was in truth giving way to the medical era, as evidenced by the continuing debate over hospitals and how to run them. The scientific era was only a distant promise, with the nod given to it in simple devices like the manual typewriter, the telephone, and the growing use of electricity.

In fact, the religious period had trailed behind the medical for many decades in the United States, until the scientific era took over. When the scientific became the predominant one, the break from the religious and medical periods was not only cemented but inescapably evident. I'd be inclined to agree with Tom Brokaw, when he hosted a program on the sixties and said that 1968 was the year that separated the past from the future. Oh, all three systems are present, but not all are equal by any means. Only one can be called an era.

Surely, understanding the change in eras is paramount to being receptive to our next step. *Downton Abbey* actually provided a tremendous wakeup call for Christianity today. It sent out warning signals to our church organizations. To hold on till there is nothing left of our inspiration, spiritual energy, and dedication would be a terrible loss. The last person out would then wearily turn off the church lights and say with a sigh, "We hung on to the bitter end." But is that the scenario our dear Leader foresaw and desired?

It's imperative to trace her writings on the subject for clues. Should we wonder if this is the right time to plunge deeply into this dilemma, we might also ask the much-quoted question: "If not us, who? If not now, when?"

So, let's look through the textbooks, and meekly, mentally, importunately ask God, divine Love, for an answer.

In speaking of her church being organized (Mis. 91), Mrs. Eddy wrote it should be a "concession to the period" (obviously the religious period). She also predicted: "But the time cometh when the religious element, or Church of Christ, shall exist alone in the affections, and need no organization to express it." (Mis. 145)

The Church of Christ is evidently spoken of in the generic sense. It's a term that covers all of Christendom and those that follow the Christ, Truth, as Jesus presented it. The Christian Science church, along with other Christian denominations, is a specific instance of that Church of Christ. She went on to say, "The real Christian compact is love for one another. This bond is wholly spiritual and inviolate." (Mis. 91) Difficult to organize (or disorganize) that love, isn't it!

There are other helpful statements such as one which refers to holding on too long to organization and thereby retarding spiritual growth. (Ret. 45) So, what was the end game or the goal that Mary Baker Eddy envisioned? What is the big picture that we need to see, and what new ways should we adopt? The answer is quite simply put in her concise statement: "Material organization is requisite in the beginning; but when it has done its work, the purely Christly method of teaching and preaching must be adopted." (Mis. 359)

We may notice she does not include the Christly method of healing, because obviously that holy activity cannot be and had not been organized.

Now, it appears we are faced with the challenge of how to transition from here to there, from organization, which is fading, to the Christly method. In one of her later interviews, the Leader of the Christian Science Movement predicted that her Church would "evolve scientifically." (My. 342)

That sounds more doable, doesn't it! To evolve isn't to arrive all at once. In fact, it means "to develop gradually." But, how do we feel about evolving?

Statements such as following may be heard:

"Why not just give up on organization and not try anything else!"

"My friends and I have had some really rough experiences in our church, and I'm tired of it."

"I've worked in church for years, and I'm just tired, period."

"I've been reading other literature that sounds close enough, and it's easier for me to understand."

It appears we are dealing with a little organizational discontent and weariness, so a distinction needs to be made.

Equating church organization with the discovery of Christian Science, or to consider these as synonymous, would impede progress. The discovery came before the organization, and should live on after it. Such a mistake might have one believing that Christian Science is disappearing even as an organization dwindles.

People tend to feel responsible for that which is entirely out of their control. An unforgettable instance of that happened in my office decades ago. I was seeing someone in the practice and the visit was an hour long. The time passed quickly, and I was surprised to look up at the clock and see it was almost 2 o'clock. When I remarked on that, the dear woman immediately exclaimed with contrition, "Oh, I'm so sorry!" We both laughed, as I reminded her that time passing was not her fault.

Likewise, no one is responsible because the times have changed, and there's no failure on anyone's part. The disappointment people feel is usually due to the passing of the remnants of the religious era. Just look at how difficult it was for the *Downton Abbey* elite to consider the fact that their old ways would no longer be viable! Our own change of eras, though it may mean a diminishing or changing form of religious organizations, does not necessarily herald the lessening of faith or search for Truth. It could mean just the opposite, as evidenced by the news that prayer has actually been increasing.

Glen would say you shouldn't kick out the rung below you on the ladder you're climbing. There's no need to denigrate organization, which has sheltered the discovery, just because we are in a new era. Nor do we need to abandon "the niceties" of living and caring for others.

There are often sound moral reasons for some of our customs—reasons such as affection and compassion. Today, society shows its caring for children and seniors in discounted tickets for travel or for events. These are our current customs of kindness. Past customs may seem antiquated but actually had a sound basis. Here is one example.

My friend Richard and I were walking along a street in Santa Barbara, where he lives, when I suddenly realized he was on the "wrong side." I'd been brought up with the custom that the man always walks on the curb side of the woman.

Having known Richard for decades, I felt quite free to request a change. "Maybe it sounds strange, but would you mind walking on the other side of me?" Immediately, he complied and replied that it was not strange at all, and that he had been brought up the same way. Then he told the following story of how he'd learned the reasoning behind such a custom.

His family was stationed in Hawaii when he was about fourteen. They were walking along a street in Honolulu, and he was being coached in manners by his dad. This included walking on the curb side of a woman. Richard told me he didn't understand why he should, but he was obedient and did so. To set the scene, perhaps you know that in Hawaii there are frequent rain showers that leave puddles on the road, and when that family was walking along there were many such puddles.

When he changed over to the side of the curb, he remarked to his family that he didn't understand the reason for this custom. At that precise moment, a car came swooshing by in a puddle and showered him with a spray of water. Being a quick learner, Richard said, "Oh! Now I see why." There really was sound logic behind that custom.

Of course, customs may be simply "transient standards." (S&H 247) Any custom of value has to have a moral or spiritual basis. Though times may change, the moral basis is what lasts and takes a new form. This comforts us when we find church buildings becoming emptied of the flock, and attached customs seem to vanish, almost overnight.

It does not appear from her writings, that Mary Baker Eddy intended to fill Christian Science churches with people. Rather did she hope to fill human hearts with the love of God and a practical understanding of the Science of Christianity. This prophecy bears that out.

If the lives of Christian Scientists attest their fidelity to Truth, I predict that in the twentieth century every Christian church in our land, and a few in far-off lands, will approximate the understanding of Christian Science sufficiently to heal the sick in his name. (Pul. 22)

Regarding "the lives of Christian Scientists," Mary Baker Eddy wrote to First Church of Christ, Scientist in New York. She spoke about goodness and rising above the question of "What am I?" to this scientific response:

I am able to impart truth, health, and happiness, and this is my rock of salvation and my reason for existing. (My. 165)

Today, there are various scenarios being offered as to how we can reach out to our brothers and sisters with the Science of Christianity, with ideas of comfort, healing and happiness.

Perhaps you've heard of the Spokane Christian Science Outreach group? With only a few members, they have talked with passersby at the local Spokane Transit Authority once a week for over seven years. They have shared comfort, encouragement, and kindness, while gifting almost 11,000 copies of

Science and Health, and other Christian Science literature.

A member of this group told me that reaching out to others with love and understanding was actually their primary purpose. It's that unselfish spirit which blesses, as it imparts "truth, health and happiness." This ministry, and that is how the participants view it, could certainly be considered a new form of church service.

A senior friend of mine, a lifelong church attendee and member, who lives on the outskirts of Los Angeles, was a member of a Christian Science branch church and then an informal group. When both of these disbanded, she was left without any organizational ties, but not without resources and her love for mankind. She joins a social group of seniors of various church denominations, who meet weekly in a park, and there she shares good and uplifting ideas with them. Church can be enacted in many ways and on many levels.

Some churches have become societies, which is rather appropriate for this scientific era, there being many societies today for various purposes. There is the National Geographic Society, also the Sierra Wildlife Society and so on. The *Manual* even implies that there may be a Christian Science society which does not hold services (p. 73). The Christian Science Publishing Society is a good example of that.

There are indeed many forms of service being explored, some out of necessity and others out of a desire to try new ways and means. This activity might increase as fear of change decreases.

Mary Baker Eddy was no stranger to change in her personal life. She went through some tumultuous personal experiences during her entire lifetime.

Her church organization likewise underwent its own changes and evolved from a small group of her students, who were members of evangelical churches, but also known as Christian Scientists. Their primary purpose in that first Christian Science Church was to "reinstate primitive Christianity and its lost element of healing."

Later her church was reorganized as The First Church of Christ, Scientist. In its description, the purpose was widened to "healing and saving the world from sin and death; thus to reflect in some degree the Church Universal and Triumphant." (Man. 16-18) The Christly method certainly fits the "Church Universal and Triumphant."

A number of events were foretold by Mrs. Eddy— future changes that would affect us all. For instance, she saw coming changes in the climate, the human body, and the manner of human reproduction.

A newer and more advanced scientific era was also envisioned by the Discoverer of Christian Science. "The education of the future will be instruction, in spiritual Science, against the material symbolic counterfeit sciences." (Mis. 61) It surely is no wonder she predicated her church would evolve scientifically. She foresaw this era!

A friend recently remarked to me that her branch church acts as though it is era proof. Of course, we can reason this out rather quickly. Though Truth is timeless and era proof, the presentation of it most certainly is not. The human condition will pass through many states and stages of development, with changing customs as it does.

Mary Baker Eddy was very conscious of the times. Speaking of her Church evolving she said, "Its government will develop as it progresses." (My. 342) A *Manual* By-Law stated her periodicals should be ably edited and "kept abreast of the times." (Man. 44) She spoke of era, period, age, and epoch. Of perfection and religion she wrote, "It will never do to be behind the times in things most essential, which proceed from the standard of right that regulates human destiny." (Mis. 232)

Renovating or repairing church buildings to make them more habitable, while not realizing that the era has changed, might put one in a position similar to that of the birdwatcher in *The Golden Prayer Puzzle*. He took note only of his own details without observing what was going on around him. Without the current context, or the understanding of our times, we could find ourselves not only impractical in today's world, but in a tenuous situation as well.

A question might be well placed at this point. If we were in a boat that had served us well, but was now leaking, and we had a vital message to transport and impart to the world, what would we do?

1. Try to attract more passengers.
2. Scold the crew and tell them to do better.
3. Make sure everyone can swim.
4. Study the message carefully, and look
for alternate transportation.

This important query leads right into the next topic regarding the right to change. Do we need permission? Questions often arise concerning the *Church Manual*, and if it wouldn't be in violation of that to evolve, or change form. Really good question!

First of all, it's important to recognize that the *Church Manual* was written for the Church, just as a car manual is written for the car. The car isn't made for its manual and neither is the Church formed for its *Manual*.

If the car evolves from a stick shift to automatic transmission, then certain parts of the car manual will no longer apply. The car is not prohibited from becoming automatic, just because the manual describes the stick shift. Changes in automobiles will continue, but the basics of care for the car and good driving rules in that manual will always apply. The same holds true for the Church and its *Manual*.

When changes occur on the religious landscape (and they can't help occurring), we will find that the literal meaning, or letter of the By-law, will be replaced with the spirit of it. This isn't a loss at all, but just a transition to a new, and often higher form, than the previous one.

For instance, what we today would term a "No stalking" By-Law, appears on p. 48 under "The Golden Rule." It insists that church members should not linger around Mrs. Eddy's home. This edict, along with an entire section on the relationship of members to their Pastor Emeritus, has been moot, obsolete, for over a hundred years in its literal sense. She hasn't been on earth, or in her home, since 1910.

However, the spirit of the By-Law could still apply to not leaning on her personality or on remarks she made to others. If we want to know her thoughts on a subject, we can look for her in her books, which is exactly the place she said we would find her. She even warned if we looked elsewhere, we would lose instead of find her.

Though the wonderful and tender recounting of her life and her comments, by people who knew her, can be valuable and inspiring, we can't lean on such information for guidance or instruction in Christian Science. Her teachings, her books, adequately fill that niche. (See *Church Manual*, p. 34)

The spirit of any By-Law will always function as a good guide even when the outer appearance changes. The idea of democracy for churches is still useful whether applied to a large congregation or a small group meeting in a home. "Wisdom, economy and brotherly love" (Man.77) will never be out of fashion nor will the "Rule for Motives and Acts," which takes one even higher than democracy, for "In Science, divine Love alone governs man." (Man. 40)

The *Manual* does not forbid change of any kind, but rather was written for and applied to the circumstance at the time and as needed. Its By-Laws "were written at different dates, and as the occasion required" (Manual 3).

The moral and spiritual laws for individuals and collectives, which the *Manual* contains, will apply though time and into eternity. "Notwithstanding the sacrilegious moth of time, eternity awaits our Church Manual,.." (My. 229) More on moths in a moment.

Taking wing: Evolving not dissolving

During the Christmas season of 2011, my brother and I spent a few weeks in Sydney, where we had grown up. (I'll explain later how that visit came about.)

We went to see our old church home, which we had attended for many years, from time spent in the Infants' Room and Sunday School, until we left in our mid-teens. That's a long time in one church, and it was a large and booming church during that period.

The Christian Science lectures sponsored by our church were likewise packed events. I well remember sitting on the stairs, in the company of other children, in the upper balcony of the large theatre in nearby Kings Cross, while the adults filled all the seats both upstairs and down.

My brother and I were surprised to find that our childhood church home had been sold, and that the members were meeting elsewhere. The building was undergoing a dramatic interior building project, while the building's exterior, considered to be of historical and cultural importance, would likely be kept intact and unchanged.

We wandered through the debris in the grand foyer—the former scene of so many happy greetings—and then saw the auditorium almost devoid of its pews, which were now stacked downstairs in the Sunday School room. Quotations from the Bible and *Science and Health* still adorned the walls. It was a rather eerie view into our past and times gone by. Our Christmastime visit was indeed like Dickens' "Ghost of Christmas Past" in *A Christmas Carol*.

This rather sobering view of our childhood church home caused deep reflection. As I prayed, it seemed clear that churches now had a new, higher pathway of service to mankind to consider. This statement, almost a lament, in *Science and Health* sounds the call to that higher form. "It is sad that the phrase *divine service* has come so generally to mean public worship instead of daily deeds." Is this implying that a weekly church service could, would, or even should transform into the divine service of daily deeds?

While still in Sydney, the thought of a butterfly flitted across my mind. It was such a beautiful concept that we might even term it a golden butterfly, for it carried a message of real worth. This is how it played out in my thinking.

Science and Health uses the analogy of a chrysalis when talking about faith advancing to spiritual understanding. "Faith is higher and more spiritual than belief. It is a chrysalis state of human thought, in which spiritual evidence, contradicting the testimony of material sense, begins to appear, and Truth, the ever-present, is becoming understood." (S&H 297)

Could it be that faith-based organizations are and have been like the chrysalis, a stage of spiritual development and even a method of protection for the soon-to-be butterfly? Ah, yes, a butterfly church could evolve from that chrysalis state. What a wonderful thought!

In researching butterflies, here is what we find. Like bees, butterflies do carry pollen to plants and flowers. They just can't carry as much, but they can carry it farther.

We also learn that a cocoon and a chrysalis are not the same thing. The caterpillar that becomes a moth spins a cocoon around itself for protection. The caterpillar that becomes a butterfly has, at a point of growth, its own hardened skin for protection, which will finally be shed. That is the chrysalis.

In this scenario of a butterfly church, it's easy to see that organization was needed at the beginning to protect the evolving church. The organized or chrysalis stage of faith was a "suffer it to be so now," as Mrs. Eddy stated. But when the butterflies are ready to emerge, to confine them further would be a great disadvantage and even danger to their progress. When no longer needed, "continued organization retards spiritual growth." (Ret. 45)

Our butterfly research all seems to fit, so far, with statements by Mary Baker Eddy. Let's go a little deeper.

The challenge is to become a productive butterfly, rather than a pesky moth, munching away in discontent, feeding on the fabric of others' good lives. The moth mentality that builds a cocoon for protection will not want to leave it behind. But the brave butterfly, not fearing to let go of what initially promoted its infant growth, has confidence in shedding that outer layer, so it can take free wing. Becoming a butterfly is an individual experience, though it could apply to a group, who feel the time is right for them to emerge. Some of the outreach efforts recounted earlier would surely fit the butterfly church description.

I'll just insert a note of reassurance here. Don't be surprised if there is a "moth attack" on your good butterfly work. It's the same resistance that any Godlike endeavor usually receives, and it can even come from the most unlikely sources, those whom you would expect to welcome the expanded view of church. The scientific evolving of church will continue, despite any resistance to it, for Mrs. Eddy prophesied it would.

A logical question could be asked at this point: What can we do to promote progress for individuals, for society, and mankind in general? There are some obvious points to consider. Keeping "the Christly method" in mind as our final goal (the butterfly church fits in well here too with that method), we can read the signs of the times and so be ready and able to take the steps required of us. We can be willing to evolve! And most importantly of all, we can ask God to show us the way. "Shepherd, show me how to go."

Over the last thirty years or so, volunteer groups have increased and are so often populated with members of Christian churches. They are dedicated to doing daily good deeds for mankind. Just from my own observation of decades, I'd say the humanitarian efforts are increasing almost in proportion as the churches are decreasing.

Perhaps one new form of the generic Church of Christ is to be found hiding in plain sight, within those groups and efforts, and not under a steeple! Brotherly and sisterly love (the Golden Rule) is found to be flourishing in unexpected ways and places. There is active agreement with Mrs. Eddy's prayer given in a poem. "My prayer some daily good to do to thine for Thee, An offering pure of Love, whereto God leadeth me." (Mis. 397)

Mere humanitarian efforts can sometimes be mistaken and fruitless, for they often begin with, and are motivated by, the human scene. Divine service to mankind, though seeing the human need, begins with God, and is led by divine Love. Furthermore, such service will always be era proof.

It will doubtless take all the unbiased, humble and receptive thought we can muster to make the transition in era. Isaiah urged (62:10) "go through the gates; prepare ye the way of the people"— even those gates of the city foursquare so that the stars of our spiritual compass may shine on our efforts and pathway. And how will we know we are making true progress? "The objects we pursue and the spirit we manifest reveal our standpoint, and show what we are winning." (S&H 239)

It will take unselfed love to share the truth with no agenda, but with a love that is for Love's sake alone. The butterflies won't be making the rounds, checking on the flowers to see how many have sprung up from their efforts. That's not in their orb, or their field of interest.

They will have one main concern, however, and that is the pollen they gather and share ("how to gather, how to sow"). It is truly their only concern, that they be wise and truthful butterflies. It will require great consecration of thought and aim to learn this divine Truth accurately, without the personal sense issue of who taught what and how, but to allow the books to be our teachers. We can be grateful that truly dedicated teachers do turn their students to the textbooks for answers. Why is this so vitally important? It's vital, because of the following warning:

Posterity will have the right to demand that Christian Science be stated and demonstrated in its godliness and grandeur, — that however little be taught or learned, that little shall be right. Let there be milk for babes, but let not the milk be adulterated. Unless this method be pursued, the Science of Christian healing will again be lost, and human suffering will increase. (Ret. 61)

Surely, it will be up to the butterfly church, as it sows seeds for the present and the future, to prevent that from happening. Yes, there are infinite possibilities for this evolving church and they will be revealed, but the love that powers the butterfly wings will need to be accompanied by the truth that sets us free. Dedicated butterflies will make sure that what they share will remain pure pollen, the pure truth.

Who can say what form our brotherhood will finally take, or what the Church Universal and Triumphant looks like. One leader in a Christian church made the comment that Christianity began in people's homes, and it would return there.

One thing is for certain. A more spiritual sense is permeating chapel walls, because faith must eventually be transformed and rise higher into spiritual understanding.

In the proportion that takes place, we'll recognize and experience the Church of Christ, the one that "shall exist alone in the affections, and need no organization to express it."

In the meantime, how beautifully symbolic that, as butterflies in the making, we carry our own protection with us rather than trying to fabricate one around us. And we will rejoice when the time comes to shed the temporary protection of the chrysalis, so we can emerge unconfined and free, ready for a higher purpose. Then, as we look around at our new world of possibilities, what do we do?

"Beholding the infinite tasks of truth, we pause, — wait on God. Then we push onward, until boundless thought walks enraptured, and conception unconfined is winged to reach the divine glory." (S&H 323)

PART FOUR

Traveling West: Divine Science

Learning life lessons through prayer

Earnest Eager could hardly believe he had traveled so far and was making the turn to go up the west river. He couldn't wait for the final phase of the journey.

Earnest was so enthused about it and knew he was talking too much but couldn't quite restrain himself. He'd heard there were all kinds of life lessons to be learned through prayer around the next bend in the river.

One thing was becoming more apparent to Earnest and it was the fact that spirituality was tremendously important. But it was not confined to any one part of society, rich or poor, educated or uneducated, or to any religion. In fact, he knew some good religious folks who were not spiritually minded at all. Then on the other hand, he had friends, who cared not one fig for church or religion and yet were very spiritually minded. Many such things were becoming clearer to him.

What Earnest didn't understand yet was if all the gold nuggets he had been amassing on his trip were going to amount to something that could even look like a goldmine. He certainly hoped so as he added more to his list from the south side journey.

There were many golden nuggets and on various topics. He loved the ideas about praying for others, including our enemies, and also what forgiveness really entailed. The golden butterfly gave him hope. He wondered just how much more he'd find on this last leg, as the boat turned the bend to travel the western side.

So, Earnest kept looking forward and outward, until suddenly he caught sight of many other vessels on the river. They were not alone. In fact, they had a lot of company!

* * * * * * * * * *

We've traveled quite a distance along the river of prayer in our exploration boat. Having found and tested the gold of prayer on the north, we then quickly rounded the next bend traveling east, where we spent the gold on ourselves. We enjoyed our communication and connection to God through prayer. It took a little longer, as we sailed south, to reach the House of Light and learn how to spend our gold on others by praying for them. Now we are poised for the western side, the fourth and final phase of this particular expedition.

The stars have been of inestimable value on our search. For instance, what value would the Word of God be unless we aligned with it? That's why the North Star is necessary to shine that light of alignment. The star of Bethlehem beckons us to follow the example of Jesus on the path of the Christ, even as the Wisemen of yore followed it. Again, what purpose would the pathway of Jesus hold for us unless we walked in it? The Southern Cross is a stark reminder of the Cross of Calvary and of the human necessity to sacrifice, give up lower ideals, for the way of true Christianity. What use would the cross be if we never sacrificed anything?

And now, we are poised and ready to let the understanding of the divine, instead of mere belief, take hold of our lives. This is the Golden Shore of Love and the Peaceful Sea of Harmony—the daystar. The night stars have retired in the presence of the light of the dawn—the dawning of truth on human thought. The daystar of divine Science has been a constant, if unacknowledged, presence.

Before his ascension, Jesus had told his followers to return to Jerusalem and wait for the arrival of that dawn, for the Holy Ghost, or divine Science. Here are his words as recounted by Paul in the Book of Acts 1:8, ". . .ye shall receive power, after that the Holy Ghost is come upon you: and ye shall be witnesses unto me both in Jerusalem, and in all Judaea, and in Samaria, and unto the uttermost part of the earth."

And here is the explanatory statement of his promise of the Pentecostal experience, which comes to each one of us as we round the city foursquare.

> The magnitude of Jesus' work, his material disappearance before their eyes and his reappearance, all enabled the disciples to understand what Jesus had said. Heretofore they had only believed; now they understood. The advent of this understanding is what is meant by the descent of the Holy Ghost, — that influx of divine Science which so illuminated the Pentecostal Day and is now repeating its ancient history. (S&H 43)

The western side of the city, divine Science, is where we all begin to really understand and not simply believe the wonderful truths we read and study. We too will receive "the influx of divine Science."

What does prayer have to do with a Science? Is it needed at the point of day dawning, when the light of understanding comes to us? Do we continually need to ask? Again, there comes the temptation to merely repeat what we know rather than to continue asking. However, prayer still has a very special function.

On the side of understanding, the petition from the Lord's Prayer: "And lead us not into temptation, but deliver us from evil" has special meaning for us. We will resist the urge to go into byways of wrong thinking or doing, as we make that request. Let us not be led astray by false teachings, false knowledge, or a false science. They may parade themselves in garments that seem more appealing, easier to understand or easier to wear, but Paul warned Timothy of them in these words:

> O Timothy, keep that which is committed to thy trust, avoiding profane and vain babblings, and oppositions of science falsely so called: Which some professing have erred concerning the faith. (1 Tim. 1:6)

By understanding life lessons, belief is being constantly replaced with understanding, just as with a child in school. Making good use of our earthly school room certainly shows the desire to understand the lessons that come with each day.

As that happens, we'll stay on track and not be led on a wrong path. God isn't sending us false information or tempting us. He isn't providing tasty tidbits from someone's metaphysical table. That's why *Science and Health* can follow up our heartfelt request with the scientific assertion, "And God leadeth us not into temptation, but delivereth us from sin, disease, and death." (S&H 17)

There truly is no possibility of gaining simpler or deeper, more meaningful metaphysics than those contained in our textbooks. We all may discover wonderful new ways of applying the basics, but the core has to remain unchanged. It can only be renewed (restored, refreshed) in our thinking, but not altered. What an amazing, infinite variety of musical compositions can be derived from a basis of just twelve notes! New melodies surface daily.

> Though our first lessons are changed, modified, broadened, yet their core is constantly renewed; as the law of the chord remains unchanged, whether we are dealing with a simple Latour exercise or with the vast Wagner Trilogy. (Ret. 81)

Humble prayer will help cancel the temptation to change the core teachings. Another reason prayer is so needed on the fourth side, of understanding the divine Science, is because of what prayer does.

> Prayer begets an awakened desire to be and do good. It makes new and scientific discoveries of God, of His goodness and power. It shows us more clearly than we saw before, what we already have and are; and most of all, it shows us what God is. (No. 39)

Prayer makes new and scientific discoveries! A startling statement for those believing that any science can stand on its own, without prayer. Speaking of new discoveries, it may seem surprising to find a fleet of boats on our river. We are not alone! There's good reason for the sudden swell in our river population, for on the western side, on the shore, are very many schoolhouses with open doors inviting us to enter. We're all prepared and eager to take classes and learn how to improve our lives. Perhaps this indicates humanity's underlying desire to understand and know Life, God.

Mary Baker Eddy's simple statement, "Earth's preparatory school must be improved to the utmost," (S&H 486) is an accepted sentiment today. Yes, so many acknowledge we're here to learn lessons—life lessons. But how shall we learn them? That is the question.

The teacher of an enrichment class for senior citizens was overheard talking in an elevator with some of her pupils. A man asked her, "Do you just teach affirmations, or do you include denials as well?" It's a popular topic. In fact, we could say the buzz word for some time now has been "affirmations." A book claiming to have found the key to getting what you want out of life lists a hundred or more affirmations to do with success, health and finances. Prayer doesn't appear to enter into the "success" equation. Neither is humility discussed because, of course, it takes humility to ask.

Now it's just as difficult to experience heavenly harmony—"as in heaven, so on earth"—without asking God questions, as it is to progress in an academic school without asking the teacher any questions. So, this last section is all about learning life lessons through prayer. We'll turn away from what the human mind wants in order to find the divine Mind's perfect plan for us all. Divine Science is an invaluable aid to students in life's classroom.

Just as the disciples waited for their Pentecostal Day to come, we may expect that same light to dawn on us and reveal just what we are learning and why.

Finding-the-subject lesson

When Glen and I moved to the top of Palomar Mountain in Southern California, we referred to our tiny home among the trees as our new classroom. We knew we were there to learn spiritual lessons. What we didn't realize was that we would also be enrolled in night school. Now, Palomar Mountain was quiet enough in the daytime, there being only about two hundred full-time residents, plus the summertime visitors, of course. You can imagine how quiet it was at night in the middle of ten wooded acres.

However, one night a telephone "went off." Yes, it sounded like an alarm clock, yet no one was calling us. Having been roused from sleep, we then talked about the preceding day and began listening for lessons in it. Then, for various reasons, we'd wake up night after night, and our school sessions would usually last a couple of hours in the dark. Sometimes, when our night school hadn't taken place for awhile, we would pray, "Dear Father, please show us our next step" and night school would occur again.

There was always a subject attached to the lessons, and if at first this seemed a negative subject, like pride, it was always corrected by something very positive, such as humility. Then of course we had to live it, which was proof we were learning it.

You may recall that Glen and I had learned the lesson on the mountain about not speculating on others' motives or even statements. If it was important enough to know, we should ask them.

This idea leads to a much larger picture. If it's important for communication and kindness' sake to understand what another means (whether we agree with them or not), how much more important it is to ask our heavenly Parent the meaning of life lessons —to understand what God is saying. So we need to ask what the lesson is. What is the subject?

Example: The red shoes

The year had to be 1967, according to my best calculations, and the lesson lasted forty years until January of 2007. No comments please at this point like, "What took you so long!" We can remember the Children of Israel wandered in the wilderness for forty years when a quicker route was available to them. It's interesting what gets in the way of learning our lessons, and why they are prolonged. In this case, I thought I knew what the lesson was.

It began when my dear parents, who were always tender of heart, wanted to buy a pair of shoes for a little girl whose mother evidently needed some help. So, my parents, the child, her mother and I all went to a department store. As my parents were giving the shoes and I had young children of my own, I became the designated shopper, trying various pairs of shoes on the child. My parents even remarked on the energy I put into this, so I redoubled my efforts under their approving gaze.

A number of pairs were rejected, and then it came to the red shoes. The little girl was enamored of them and said she wanted those. Feeling these weren't practical, I encouraged the party to put their support behind a serviceable pair of brown shoes. Over the child's disappointment, the brown shoes were purchased. All seemed to end well.

However, the red shoes began to haunt me. Now and then they would pop up and I would sigh, "All she wanted was a pair of red shoes." This went on for literally decades. From time to time and for no apparent reason, there were the red shoes, dancing in the background, and that nagging, sad feeling that I hadn't been loving enough. I also chastised myself for any pride I had at the time, due to my parents' approval.

Each time the shoes accused me, I tried to remind myself that it was just a good lesson and would teach me to love more. I would take the red shoe episode out my mental files, where it had been placed under "Auriel's misdeeds," and put it into the "opportunities to love" folder. However, the red shoes would never stay put. The next time the thought came up, there they were again in the "misdeeds" category. I mourned over this and wished I could have done better, until something very unusual happened.

In January of 2007, I awakened rather early one morning with some ideas for a talk on parenting. It would be good to add a section on helping children to make better choices.

Then quite suddenly, I mentally saw a vignette in front of me almost like a replay of a movie but with the plot now clear. I "saw" that mother and child, though this wasn't a physical recognition, because I could never recall what they looked like. No, this was a metaphysical uncovering, because instantly came the knowledge that poor choices were being made in that little family. It was now clear that we were not there simply to get the child what she liked, or even what she needed, but to help her understand and make better choices too.

During that period of time, and as her only pair of shoes, the brown would be much more suitable for all occasions than the red. With this revelation, the vision faded and the sorrow over the red shoes faded with it. I'd had the wrong subject (lack of love) all those years and as soon as the correct topic—helping children to make better choices—was present, then that event came to mind as an example of it.

Christ Jesus told us, in a parable of the tares and wheat (Matthew 13), not to pull up the tares until we can distinguish them from the wheat. In my haste to berate myself for lack of love, I didn't recognize the wheat of that experience. The whole process could have been shortened by asking God for the lesson, namely, that wisdom is just as necessary as love. God is Love, but God is also divine Mind, the intelligence of the universe, and both must be expressed. The red shoes are now comfortably and permanently settled in their new mental folder under "wisdom and love," subtitled, "helping children to make better choices."

Sometimes there are a few similar events in a day that come under the same heading. One morning, it appeared as though the family of a friend was relying unnecessarily on her. By mid-day I became disappointed, when someone didn't so something for me that I had expected them to do. By the evening, another individual told of all the people who wouldn't help her.

When the day's subject became obvious—the need to lean on God—then my own disappointment disappeared. It was simply part of a lesson that reminded me to lean more on God and to help others do likewise. Another good day in earth's preparatory school!

The humility lesson

"The human mind is opposed to God and must be put off, as St. Paul declares," states *Science and Health* page 151. Why this opposition? Because the human mind has its own agenda, its own desires to pursue, rather than the plan of the divine Mind. It balks at giving up human will for the divine will, and would rather substitute good sounding phrases for the humility of asking, listening and following obediently what divine Love is requiring of us.

Mrs. Eddy says humility is a requirement for healing and "must be had to understand our textbook." (Mis. 356) She makes strong statements on the subject and some may be a little hard to take. (But no rushing through this part, please!) Let's look under the surface of *Miscellany* page 165.

Of two things fate cannot rob us; namely, of choosing the best, and of helping others thus to choose. But in doing this the Master became the servant. The grand must stoop to the menial. There is scarcely an indignity which I have not endured for the cause of Christ, Truth, and I returned blessing for cursing. The best help the worst; the righteous suffer for the unrighteous; and by this spirit man lives and thrives, and by it God governs.

Does that seem just—the righteous suffer for the unrighteous? No, it may not be just, but justice is not the topic here. The spirit of humility is. The human mind objects to this, concentrates on the possible injustice, not humility. It even calls into question the enduring love of our Father-Mother, rather than face the lesson, though by humility we will thrive!

Now, let's try this garment on for size. It's a designer label called "humiliation," and is found in *No and Yes* on page 39. Please note that it is custom tailored for each one of us.

> Prayer can neither change God, nor bring His designs into mortal modes; but it can and does change our modes and our false sense of Life, Love, and Truth, uplifting us to Him. Such prayer humiliates, purifies, and quickens activity, in the direction that is unerring.

Humiliates? That sounds pretty awful doesn't it! But successful prayer really does humiliate us. It humbles (lowers) us in our own eyes and perhaps even in the eyes of others.

Now, with only two quotations we have gained the possibility of taking part in menial tasks, indignities, suffering for the unrighteous and humiliation. Need we wonder more why the human mind is not prone to learning humility?

It's either time for recess in "earth's preparatory school" (skip the lesson altogether) or work hard metaphysically to make the situation disappear. In the following instance, however, neither option was taken.

Example: A questionable promotion

A woman, who was head of her department, with many years of work experience, assigned tasks to a newcomer, a young man fresh out of high school. After five years, he more or less became her protégé. Then, for another five years, she trained him further in many facets of the work.

One day the news came that the woman's supervisor was going to retire, and rumor had it that the young man would be promoted to that position. What a potentially humiliating situation that appeared to be! But the woman had grown up with an understanding of Christian Science. So, when a family member suggested the new situation could turn out to be a blessing (if some patience was applied), she decided not to react. She would wait on God and listen to Him as well as she could. That desire to hear God became her patient prayer.

Well, the young man was indeed promoted to the position of being the woman's supervisor, and the one to whom she would report. Now, he would write reviews on her performance instead of the other way round.

There was some logic to this decision, however, because the woman had not wanted that position (it included an expertise in which she was neither educated nor interested) and the young man was well suited for it. But one may wonder: Did it have to be that specific individual in the new position and not someone else? Couldn't it have been less embarrassing for her? Couldn't divine Love have arranged this in a different fashion? In actual fact, divine Love had all the bases covered, though it took almost a year of patient waiting for the woman to recognize the benefits. The light of understanding finally dawned on her, and the Golden Shore of Love came into view.

Because the young man knew the intricacies of the woman's department, having been trained by her, he could support her ways and means in the work far better than could a newcomer, who was less knowledgeable. He was also much more objective than his predecessor, so the atmosphere in the office was improved. Like the Peaceful Sea of Harmony, a greater peace flowed into that office and into her life.

The woman admits that it sometimes still feels a little strange reporting to someone who used to report to her, but she also acknowledges that this was the best outcome. She has no regrets, hurt feelings or embarrassment over it. What a great lesson in humility that was. She obviously passed with flying colors!

The joy lesson

Just in case we are inclined to think that spiritual lessons do not include happy times and answers to desires other than basic spiritual needs, I'm including this lesson. Perhaps, to avoid some kind of prohibition on joy, Mrs. Eddy tells us this about pleasure. "And pleasure is no crime except when it strengthens the influence of bad inclinations or lessens the activities of virtue." (Mis. 362)

When we think more deeply about this, joy is a spiritual need that God does fill. The sackcloth of religious or joyless piety is not the required garb for a sincere Christian. In fact, Mary Baker Eddy agreed with Rev. Dr. Talmage that there are, "wit, humor, and enduring vivacity among God's people." (Mis. 117) As is stated, on page 113, "We have nothing to fear when Love is at the helm of thought, but everything to enjoy on earth and in heaven."

This is such a happy lesson to learn and relearn and learn again. God has not only duty, but a joyful purpose for us all.

I ended a poem titled, "A Holy Presence" published in *The Christian Science Journal* of December, 1998 with this stanza.

> But Love divine has greater plan
> Than our duty well fulfilled;
> It's joy that runneth over,
> And o'er us will be spilled.

I have to admit that the poem, being written only a few years after Glen's passing, was more of a hope than a fact in my life at that time. However, the truth of the poem was vividly born out years later when a long-standing desire of mine was met in quite an amazing way.

Example: The pot of gold

Even to me, this particular desire looked rather non-essential or even frivolous, so I was rather sure it wouldn't be right to ask divine Love about it. The desire was to visit my native country of Australia, Sydney's Bronte Beach in particular, and with my brother. We had lived, swum and surfed together there during the years prior to leaving that country.

I'd been back only once with my daughter, in 2006, after a 50 year absence. She had generously shared tickets with me, and that trip was wonderful, but I had little time to spend at my childhood haunts. So now, after that visit, the idea of swimming at Bronte again with my brother John, my best friend growing up, sounded rather heavenly. I even mentioned it to him a couple of times but only in passing. I'd been putting all my time, energy and resources towards the publishing efforts and placing books into prisons and VA hospitals. I was not about to use precious book funds on a trip for myself.

Then in 2011, the totally unexpected happened. A woman I knew only slightly came to visit me. She deposited a rather bulky gold paper sack on my living room floor and told me she wanted me to have whatever it was, while she still had it to give. A mystery and a surprise awaited me! In the sack lay heaps of crumpled bills (purposely done to make it look more of a treasure find). After piles of 5s, 10s, and 20s were spread around and counted, the total came to $2,000. How could I accept this and why?

She explained that Glen had done such wonderful healing work for her family, which included saving her life and that of her son, that she wanted to show her gratitude. (Those healings had to have taken place about twenty-five years prior to this.)

You can imagine (or maybe you can't, if you know me) that I was speechless. Furthermore, as my mind was racing towards all possible scenarios of book giving, she added that she'd like me to spend it on myself. Oh!

The visit took place on a Friday. I deposited my pot of gold into the bank, while I gratefully cogitated, over the weekend, on this windfall. The following Monday, out of the blue, my brother called with a plan he had. How would I like to go to Sydney with him at Christmas, and just pay for my own airfare. He would pick up all the food and accommodation expenses. Well, it just so happened I had the fare sitting in the bank, waiting!

That however, was only the beginning of the saga. He had noticed online, when planning the trip, that there was special compensation for the Australian military, who had been in Japanese prison camps during the war. We were able to look into it when in Sydney and secure that generous gift from the Australian government, their "ex gratia" (out of kindness) payment, for our stepmother. Our own wonderful mother had passed on many years before and our dad had remarried. It was this dear lady who urged him to write his book. So, decades after my dad's passing, this gift was given to his widow, as was the gift given to me years after Glen's passing, and by a woman whose husband had likewise been gone many years. Time evidently meant nothing. The provision, the gold, multiplied. It was almost like the widow's store in the Bible being replenished. Many people were blessed by that visit to Sydney.

Did we swim at Bronte Beach during those three weeks? Yes, but not for long as it was so cold that month, though it was summer. What we did, however, was to live like children again in the moment, day by day, and we brought the past up to the present. When we think of Sydney, it's in "now" time.

These were all beautiful lessons for which I'm so, so grateful. And that's the story of how I came to see the golden butterfly in Sydney. Yes, the western side has been alight with spiritual understanding. It is during this period of progress that our thinking makes the change over from belief to the actual understanding of divine Science. Now, we are ready for the point.

The point is Christian Science

Under the heading "Divine Science" Mrs. Eddy explained that it is "another name for Christian Science, the cognomen of all true religion, the quintessence of Christianity, that heals disease and sin and destroys death!" (Mis. 336)

A cognomen is a surname, which indicates we are on the right track, and that divine Science is the family name, the general title, of which Christian Science is the specific. Our travel along the side of divine Science has included many lessons pertaining to the underlying, invisible laws of good that govern the spiritual universe. Life lessons learned and discerned have fortified us. Our feet are more firmly planted now on the solid ground of understanding, not the shifting sands of belief. We have been beckoned to the Golden Shore of Love, because Love is both our basis and our goal.

Sailing along on the Peaceful Sea of Harmony, we're now ready to touch the western point of the city, which is explained this way.

> Christian Science, which to-day and forever interprets this great example and the great Exemplar. (S&H 577)

Christian Science will live up to its surname of divine Science and make that family name illustrious!

The perfect "app"

Mrs. Eddy explained how important it is to meet the human need and even described the Lord's Prayer as one "that covers all human needs." Likewise, she described Christian Science as an application to the human scene. Under the paragraph heading "Scientific terms" we find the following on page 127 of *Science and Health*:

> The terms Divine Science, Spiritual Science, Christ Science or Christian Science, or Science alone, she employs interchangeably, according to the requirements of the context. These synonymous terms stand for everything relating to God, the infinite, supreme, eternal Mind. It may be said, however, that the term Christian Science relates especially to Science as applied to humanity.

"Science as applied to humanity" has to be the perfect application, or "app" in today's usage. The temptation may be to stay with the surname, the general or divine side, without getting to the specifics, the point of the Science.

Christian Science is the specific application of Science, and is the perfect "app" for humanity in meeting their needs. But just as a misunderstood phone app would lose its appeal and usefulness, there is danger in not having an accurate understanding of our application called Christian Science.

Divine Science is not compromised by specifically applying its rules to the human scene, anymore than the principle of mathematics is compromised by applying its rules to the numbers on the chalkboard. Being scientific simply means we understand the rules enough to apply them. Jesus was not oblivious to human needs, for he met human needs. Yes, he fully used (though he didn't specifically explain) that app for the human scene.

If we speak to others of the possible loss of Christian Science, the quick answer will often be given that it's impossible to lose Christian Science. That's actually not true, because Mrs. Eddy warns us of it three times.

Reasoning this out, we find that God cannot lose what belongs to Him, and divine Science certainly does belong to Him. But it's possible to lose our understanding of it. And more specifically, it is possible to lose the application of that Science to humanity—the app termed Christian Science. This has been mentioned in part already.

There are many steps to prevent such a loss. Mary Baker Eddy provides three warnings (we could call them fire-walls) to protect the discovery. These appear in Man. 43:21, Ret. 61: 26 and in *Science and Health*, 410:23. Three temptations to watch for and overcome!

The Lord's Prayer, put into practice, will save us from each of those temptations and help reverse and efface any wrong work. There is always the opportunity to make radical changes for the better, and to turn towards the light.

Choosing the light

It's always a matter of choosing to follow the light of Truth. The statement that the Lord's Prayer "covers all human needs" sounds almost too good to be true. But, is it?

Here is an example of what happened to my dear Glen, when he and others were on the way to speak to a large meeting of Christian Science youth. The carload of seasoned Christian Scientists was leaving Chicago for that one-day event.

The trip was proceeding well, when someone remarked with some concern, "Oh, Glen, did you know that the knee of your trousers is becoming threadbare?"

No, he hadn't noticed that, but others in the car then verified that was the case. There was nothing to be done about it, so Glen turned his whole attention to the event of the day and his part in it. He was the last speaker and had assembled five or six important points to make in his talk.

As it happened, the speakers before him, without knowing it, proceeded to take away his points one at a time in their own talks, until finally only one point remained. There was one more speaker to go, and strangely enough, that speaker took his last point. Glen was virtually left without any talk to be given or points to be made! I'm sure you can imagine that scene was a speaker's nightmare.

Glen told me how he turned so vigorously, so importunately, to God for an answer and one came to him. He felt impelled to talk about the Lord's Prayer, which he did spontaneously with joy and inspiration. The ideas came flooding in. He didn't even recall later exactly what was said, but he and the audience were transported. They truly felt the spirit of it wash over them. Happily, it was a very successful meeting for all concerned.

A couple of days later, Glen took the trousers in to the local tailor for invisible mending. At least, he hoped that could be accomplished. The tailor looked them over carefully and almost impatiently asked Glen why on earth he had brought those pants in. There was absolutely nothing wrong with them. They were in perfect condition! (Talk about a case of invisible mending!)

What happened here? Glen turned away from the human need of the threadbare pants. He turned away from the situation he was faced with—the loss of each aspect of his talk. He chose to follow the light of Truth instead. He prayed and then obeyed what came to him—to speak about the Lord's Prayer, trusting that the words would be there. And they were! That prayer covered all of his needs.

Surely, all the dedicated prayers uttered through the last few centuries helped pave the way for Jesus' prayer to be seen in a new light. In 1875, this prayer was presented again to the world, and this time with its spiritual sense. This is not an addition to the prayer, but the scientific translation of it.

The western point of the city foursquare is like a magnifying glass. It gives the specifics and enlarges our understanding of the prayer that unites all Christian churches. Let's note the emphasis that Mary Baker Eddy places on two of the petitions.

> All Christian churches have one bond of unity, one nucleus or point of convergence, one prayer, — the Lord's Prayer. It is matter for rejoicing that we unite in love, and in this sacred petition with every praying assembly on earth, — "Thy kingdom come. Thy will be done in earth, as it is in heaven. (Pul. 22)

Loving to do God's will would surely eliminate any temptation to do man's will. Love keeps us safe.

We are now approaching the goldmine where we hope to reach the "heart of prayer." Instructions are given for seekers to enter the "quiet sanctuary of earnest longings" silently and humbly. Shutting out all extraneous thoughts, we commune with our Father-Mother, God. (S&H 15)

Our Father which art in heaven,
Our Father-Mother God, all-harmonious,

Hallowed be Thy name.
Adorable One.

Thy kingdom come.
Thy kingdom is come; Thou art ever-present.

Thy will be done in earth, as it is in heaven.
*Enable us to know, — as in heaven, so on
earth, — God is omnipotent, supreme.*

Give us this day our daily bread;
*Give us grace for to-day; feed the famished
affections;*

And forgive us our debts, as we forgive our
debtors.
And Love is reflected in love;

And lead us not into temptation, but deliver us
from evil;
*And God leadeth us not into temptation, but
delivereth us from sin, disease, and death.*

For Thine is the kingdom, and the power, and
the glory, forever.
*For God is infinite, all-power, all Life, Truth,
Love, over all, and All.*

As our boat trip concludes and we glide back to the north landing, we'll review some of what we have learned of prayer. Each time, it was important to "get the point" before continuing on to the next side.

Prayer was aligning with the north point, the Word of Life, Truth and Love, under the North Star, in the Psalms of David. He prayed, "Teach me thy way, O Lord. I will walk in thy truth." (86:11) And he stated the reason: "Thy word is a lamp unto my feet, and a light unto my path." (119:105)

The point of the east revealed that Christ is the spiritual idea of God. As shown by a star, Jesus arrived as "the human herald of Christ, Truth." (S&H vii) His prayer made the forever connection of a child to its heavenly Parent, proving that Christ is also the spiritual idea of sonship.

The light of the Southern Cross illumined the point of Christianity— the necessity of sacrifice and prayers for mankind. The Golden Rule shines here!

The western point, which is Christian Science, provides the Lord's Prayer with its spiritual sense, and explains how this prayer can heal instantaneously. (S&H 16)

Finally, at the end of our prayer expedition, we'll be celebrating the fact that we may and must turn to the divine Mind for answers. We'll promise to keep our sacred communication with God safe for ourselves and for others. This is our goldmine, the gold of prayer, that Christ Jesus gave us.

Golden Glimpses

Earnest Eager left the boat with such a sense of buoyancy about his prayer search. He had been successful in finding the gold of prayer!

It had been there all along in the Guidebook, and the Key book unlocked the spiritual meaning of it. Each of the gold nuggets he'd found was needed to put it all together. They were the specific pieces of the puzzle, and now he had the big picture too!

The mystery of the little town, with its rural surroundings, was partially solved. Earnest realized it was in the shape of a diamond, with connecting bridges to the mainland at each of point of the diamond. That seemed so perfect! It showed there is always access to the little town with its big ideas. No matter at what point you enter, one can still go round as many times as necessary.

Earnest finally boarded the plane at the airstrip on the outskirts of town. As it soared upward, so did his kind heart. He saw new vistas with untold possibilities for service to mankind. Yes, he now had something of great value to share with other seekers, and Earnest promised himself he would!

* * * * * * * * * *

Perhaps you've made notes and observations, and found your own golden nuggets during this boat ride on the river of prayer. I hope it has been just as helpful to your path, as it was to Glen's and mine. Some of these unfoldments came to me after Glen had left the scene, but I've always felt we were both still learning these same life lessons. The journey hasn't always been easy, but worthwhile endeavors rarely are.

Here are some of the high points that have helped me and perhaps you too.

- Earnest Eager had the right spirit. Being both earnest and eager is vital to the spiritual journey, but so is exchanging the velocity of impetuosity for the calm of waiting patiently on God to reveal our path each day.

- Mary Baker Eddy wrote, "Humanity advances slowly out of sinning sense into spiritual understanding; unwillingness to learn all things rightly, binds Christendom with chains." (S&H 95) Humility would mean relinquishing the fragmented views of Gerald Generic and Spencer Specific, in order to learn "all things rightly."

- The selfishness of a Selby Selfish can and should be diminished to the size of a pea and blown away by the winds of inner change, a change of heart and character.

- And Colin Collector, who has resided with us for some time, is no longer a welcome guest. That habit takes up too much mental and physical space. "The advancing stages of Christian Science are gained through growth, not accretion; idleness is the foe of progress." (Mis. 206)

The human experience is full of tremendous lessons. We find that humility, as well as other graces of Spirit, will be learned on increasingly higher levels. Christ Jesus gave us the lesson plan, and Christian Science describes and interprets the spiritual laws behind this plan to eradicate sin, disease and death.

However, it's not enough to know or simply acknowledge the unreality of that trio of errors, for we're required to prove it. For that purpose, Jesus also gave us the Lord's Prayer to cover "all human needs" and showed us by example the path in which we should walk.

Divine Love helps us every step of the way to understand and dwell in "the kingdom of God" which is ever present. How do we specifically describe this kingdom, or divine consciousness, which belongs to God? It's the kingdom of heaven—"the reign of harmony in divine Science"—and is won by degrees as we advance in the most important subjects in life's school. (S&H 590)

Science and Health makes those subjects very clear on page 248:

> Let unselfishness, goodness, mercy, justice, health, holiness, love — the kingdom of heaven — reign within us, and sin, disease, and death will diminish until they finally disappear.

Each step of progress shows us more of heaven on earth until the new heaven and new earth are our only realities. The gold of prayer, the golden prayer, reveals its precious, spiritual secret and takes us the whole way!

For ordering and author information
please visit the Mountaintop website:
www.MountaintopPublishing.com

Printed in Great Britain
by Amazon